FROM PAIN

TO

PURPOSE

FROM PAIN TO PURPOSE

THE DIGNITY OF PERSONAL NEED

THE PATH AND PRACTICE OF EVOLUTIONARY LOVE

...

From Conscious Evolution 1.0 to Conscious Evolution 2.0

One Mountain, Many Paths: Oral Essays
Volume Three

DR. MARC GAFNI AND
BARBARA MARX HUBBARD

Copyright © 2025 Center for World Philosophy and Religion

All rights reserved.

No part of this book may be used or reproduced in any manner whatsoever without written permission except in the case of brief quotations embodied in critical articles or reviews.

No part of this book may be reproduced, or stored in a retrieval system, or transmitted in any form or by any means, electronic, mechanical, photocopying, recording, or otherwise, without express written permission of the publisher.

All brand names and product names used in this book are trademarks, registered trademarks, or trade names of their respective holders.
For additional information and press releases please contact CWPR Publishing.

Author: Marc Gafni and Barbara Marx Hubbard
Title: From Pain to Purpose
From Conscious Evolution 1.0 to Conscious Evolution 2.0

Identifiers: ISBN 979-8-88834-056-1 (electronic)
ISBN 979-8-88834-055-4 (paperback)

© 2025 Marc Gafni

Edited by Kristina Amelong, Paul Kwamme, and David Cicerchi

World Philosophy and Religion Press, St. Johnsbury, VT
in conjunction with

https://worldphilosophyandreligion.org

JOIN THE REVOLUTION!

CONTENTS

EDITORIAL NOTE ABOUT AUTHORSHIP, EDITING, AND THE RADICAL CONTEXT FOR THIS SERIES	X
LOVE OR DIE: LOCATING OURSELVES	XXII
ABOUT THIS BOOK	XXXVIII

CHAPTER 1   STEPPING INTO A MIGHTY EVOLUTIONARY JOURNEY

Meditation on the Evolutionary Impulse Within	1
We Pray to the Infinity of Intimacy	2
The Holy and the Broken Hallelujah	4
Pointing-Out Instruction for Prayer	4
Prayers to the Infinity of Intimacy	6
Evolutionary Testament of Co-Creation	7
We Are Inspiring a Planetary Pentecost	9
A Kabbalistic Story of Divine Calling	13
Letting the Ego Flower Into Your Unique Self	17

CHAPTER 2   BEAUTY AND THE BEAST: BREAKING THE SPELL OF ORDINARY LOVE

Place Attention on the Heart	19
We Are Holding the Good News	20
Intimacy Means We Are Awake and Erotic	22
We Are Held by the Divine	24
Taking the Lid Off for Love	25
Get the Power of Unique Self Symphony	29
The Beast: A Story of Posturing and Rejecting the Rose	31
Reality Is a Love Story: The Deepest Story of Reality	33
Breaking the Spell of Ordinary Love.	34
What is a Real Unique Self Symphony?	35

The Pseudo-Unique Self Symphony	35
Awakening in Love Now	37
We Need a Story that is Equal to Our Power	38

CHAPTER 3   REALITY INTENDED YOUR UNIQUE GIFT

Imagine Going the Whole Way	40
Step Outside of Our Narcissism	41
Reality Hears Me	43
If We Don't Thank God for Our Greatness, Who Will?	46
Giving Your Unique Gift	50
No One Evolves Beyond Ego	51
A Story About Unique Gift: Slipping Your Envelope Under the Door	52
You Identify Your Unique Gift	57

CHAPTER 4   ATTUNING AND RESPONDING TO OUTRAGEOUS LOVE IN A SELF-ORGANIZING UNIVERSE

Outrageous Love Drives Everything	59
Your Personal Quality Participates in God's Personal Quality	62
Embodied Awareness of Outrageous Love: Feeling the Whole Story of Creation	65
Evolutionary Chakra Meditation	66
The Universe is Perfectly Attuned for Life	66
Responding to a Politics of Devolution with a Politics of Evolution	70
To Life! The Story of Yankele	74
To Face Existential Threat, You Have to Feel Outrageous Love	77

CHAPTER 5   OUR SIX CORE ESSENTIAL HUMAN NEEDS

The Wedding Day of the Essential Self with the Universal Self	79
There Is No Contradiction Between Our Personal Needs and Evolutionary Needs	80
Personal Needs Meet Our Evolutionary Needs	82
Our Emergence as an Evolutionary Human	84
We Must Meet Our Six Core Essential Needs	87
Our True Need Is to Play a Larger Game	92

CHAPTER 6 EVOLUTION IS LOVE IN ACTION

Attuning to Your Unique Gifts in the Symphony	95
Are You Needed by the Unique Self Symphony, or Are We Just Making it Up?	96
Prayer is a Realization of the Intimate Universe	97
Who Are You? The Unique Self Response	98
Planet Earth Is Giving Birth to a Co-Evolving Humanity	100
The Intimate Universe is a Synergistic Universe	103
God Needs Us	104

CHAPTER 7 REFLECTIONS ON *CONVERSATIONS WITH GOD* AND OUTRAGEOUS LOVE

Awakening Dharma: Resonance and Planetary Evolution	107
From Broken *Hallelujah* to Evolutionary *Dharma*: Reclaiming the Divine	108
Confessions of Greatness for Planetary Awakening	111
We Get to Fall in Love Again and Again	113
Welcoming Neale Donald Walsch: Conversations with God Within	113
From Doctrine to Discovery: Awakening the Sacred Within	114
Highly Evolved Beings Are Partners in Humanity's Transmogrification	118
A Sacred Secret Within Us All	120
Not an Uncommon Dialogue	121
Messianic Conversation and Embracing the Conversation with God	122
The Holy Tipping Point: Just One Blink Away from Total Awakening	123
The Power of Self-Selection and Mirroring Global Change	125
No One Else Can Have Your Experience	126
When Everything Is Great, Then What?	127
Not Creating, but Remembering: The Essence of Divine Awareness	128
Neale's Blessing	129
Marc's Blessing	130

CHAPTER 8   THE WOUND AND THE AWAKENING: TRANSFORMING PAIN INTO INTIMACY

Tapping into the Wounding of Separation	131
Enlightenment Means the Wound Is Not Unconscious in Us	133
From Ego to Essence	139
My Wound Is the Intention of the LoveIntelligence of Cosmos	143

CHAPTER 9   THE KEYS TO ACTIVATING EVOLUTIONARY LOVERS

Our Heart's Desire is for More Love	150
Evolving the Lineages	151
We Live in a World of Broken Hearts	153
The First Key: The Activation of the New Identity	156
The Second Key: My New Identity is Rooted in a New Worldview	159
The Third Key: Activating Evolutionary Practice in a Profound and Deep Way	162
The Fourth Key: Wheel of Co-Creation 2.0	164
The Fifth Key: Activating an Evolutionary Community	164

CHAPTER 10   THE GLORY OF THE WOUND: TRANSFORMING PAIN INTO PURPOSE

My Eyes Have Seen the Glory of the Wound	166
We Are Not Wounded by Accident	167
We Are Designed to Have a Flaw in Our Design	168
Life Is Designed to Be a Misfit	169
A Call for Wounding to Rise Up in Creativity	172
Our Wound Changes Based on Who We Experience Ourselves to Be	175
Extend Your Hand and Feel the One Wound, the One Love	176

INDEX   **182**

EDITORIAL NOTE ABOUT AUTHORSHIP, EDITING, AND THE RADICAL CONTEXT FOR THIS SERIES

ORAL ESSAYS FROM THE ONE MOUNTAIN, MANY PATHS WEEKLY BROADCAST

This volume is part of the Oral Essays library, a series of lightly edited, compiled transcripts of oral teachings given by Dr. Marc Gafni and the late Barbara Marx Hubbard in their weekly online broadcast, *One Mountain, Many Paths,* which they co-founded in 2017. Originally called an "Evolutionary Church," *One Mountain, Many Paths* became a key venue for the articulation of an inspired and deeply grounded new Story of Value in response to the meta-crisis. Marc and Barbara—together with Zak Stein,[1] Kristina Kincaid, Ken Wilber, Sally Kempton, Lori Galperin, Aubrey Marcus and dozens of other thought-leaders over the years—began to articulate what they call a World Philosophy and World Religion[2] as a context for our diversity.

---

1   Zak, together with Ken Wilber, has been Marc's primary intellectual partner and an initiate lineage holder in CosmoErotic Humanism.

2   This project is grounded in four core organizational frameworks: 1) The Center for World Philosophy and Religion, co-founded by Marc Gafni, Zachary Stein, Sally Kempton, and Ken Wilber, and chaired over the years by John P. Mackey, Barbara Marx Hubbard, Aubrey Marcus, Gabrielle Anwar and Shareef Malnik, Carrie Kish and Adam Bellow, and Kathleen J. Brownback. 2) The Office for the Future, chaired by Stephanie Valcke and Ivan Bossyut. 3) The World Philosophy and Religion Press, founded and chaired by Aubrey Marcus, together with Marc Gafni and Zachary Stein. 4) The Foundation for Conscious Evolution, founded by Barbara Marx Hubbard and currently chaired by Peter

Until Barbara's passing in 2019, she and Marc transmitted teachings together as evolutionary partners and "whole mates," weaving together insights and transmissions from their decades of practice, study, teaching, and activism into a synergy of wisdom, a grounded vision for future policy across all sectors of society.

Much of the Dharma material below comes directly from Marc, so it was originally all in quotation marks—but that looked a little odd. So per his suggestion we removed them, and the reader should consider the paragraphs on the next several pages as one extended quote from him. We are joyfully grateful to Marc for the clarity of his Dharma, the elegance and "second simplicity" of this language, and the mad, Outrageous Love with which he transmits his teachings.

Barbara and Marc called the mission of *One Mountain* "a Planetary Awakening in Evolutionary Love Through Unique Self Symphonies." We are an evolutionary community with a deeply grounded, radically alive, and "post-tragic" revolutionary spirit. We are activating a new humanity and awakening as a new species: *Homo amor*, the fulfillment of *Homo sapiens*.

One Mountain is committed to articulating a Story of Value that can become the ground for the new society that must be birthed in response to the meta-crisis. We recognize that we are living at a pivotal moment in history. In this "time between stories," the great moral imperative is to tell the new Story of Value. It is ours to do, personally and collectively, with great trembling and ecstatic joy.

FROM DOGMA TO DHARMA: ETERNAL AND EVOLVING FIRST PRINCIPLES AND FIRST VALUES

The teachings are grounded in decades of deep study across many wisdom traditions. Over the years, week by week, these teachings were

---

Fiekowsky. For a complete list of key leadership, see the Office for the Future website, www.officeforthefuture.com.

incrementally developed within the framework of the *One Mountain, Many Paths* broadcast. We often refer to these teachings as *Dharma*.

This word was originally used in lineage traditions to refer to something like universal law. This is a crucial realization: just as there is universal law in mathematical value, there is also a sense of universal law in ethics and value.

Historically, Dharma often devolved into unchanging dogma. Evolution was ignored, and the natural process of Dharma evolution became disconnected from its deep, eternal context. The weakness of the word Dharma is that too often it did not include the evolving insights of the sciences, it confused local cultural truths with universal truths, and it used words like "eternal," as in "eternal Tao," as opposed to words like "evolution."

Eternal came to mean unchanging, and that kind of thinking often led to overly ethnocentric readings of Dharma. Local systems would claim their religious and cultural insights as immutable, which stood in the way of the emergence of a genuine world Story of Value that is real, inherent to Cosmos, and backed by the Universe—even as it is also always evolving.

Or, as we often say, "eternal value is evolving value. The eternal Tao is the evolving Tao."

We have shown that, emergent from profound insights in the "interior sciences," eternal does not mean unchanging in time; it means what we call the deeper Field of ErosValue that is beneath culture, geography, and history, which lives beneath all individual and collective values, and beneath time and space itself.

As such, we have gradually transitioned from the term Dharma to the term *Value*, in the sense of the Field of Value that lives beneath all values. This Field of Value discloses as First Principles and First Values embedded in a Story of Value.

Indeed, as the interior sciences knew and the exterior sciences imply, Reality arises in a Field of ErosValue in which an entire set of mathematical, musical, molecular, moral, and mystical values are the very ground of all being. That Field of Value is eternal—the true ground of the Good, True and Beautiful—even as it is evolving.

But of course, it is equally critical not just to talk about evolving value, but to ground the evolving value in its true nature, the eternal Field of First Principles and First Values, always reaching for ever-more life, ever-more love, ever-more care, ever-more depth, ever-more uniqueness, ever-more intimate communion, and ever-more transformation.

As such, when we refer to the word Dharma, which still appears in these texts together with the word value, we refer to an evolving Dharma grounded in an *eternal and evolving* Field of Value. Indeed, eternity and evolution are two faces of the whole, opposites joined at the hip, that characterize the nature of our Cosmos in virtually all of its expressions.

It's in these terms that we ground a robust world philosophy that integrates the validated, leading-edge insights of premodern traditional wisdom, modern wisdom, and more recent postmodern insights, weaving them together into a new whole greater than the sum of its parts.

This new whole is a shared Story of Value rooted in First Principles and First Values that are both eternal and evolving.

These First Principles and First Values of Cosmos are woven together into a new Story of Value as a context for our diversity, a new Universe Story. This new Story gives us the best possible responses we have to the mystery, and to the great questions:

- Who am I? Who are we?
- Where am I? Where are we?
- What should I do? What should we do?

It is only through such a shared Universe Story—a narrative of identity and ethos as a context for our blessed diversity—that we can realize how what unites is so much greater than what divides us.

Only a new Story of Value will allow us to both respond to the meta-crisis and participate together in birthing the most true, good, and beautiful world that we already know is possible.

THIS ORAL ESSAYS SERIES IS AN ENTRYWAY TO THE GREAT LIBRARY OF COSMOEROTIC HUMANISM

This Oral Essays series is part of the overarching project of the Great Library at the Center for World Philosophy and Religion, led by Dr. Marc Gafni, together with Dr. Zak Stein. The aim of the Great Library project is to articulate a robust and comprehensive new Story of Value, CosmoErotic Humanism, in the form of dozens of well-researched and extensively footnoted academic works.

Our vision is to provide the philosophical framework that will be vital for navigating humanity through this time of immense crisis and transformation.

To begin your journey into CosmoErotic Humanism, we tenderly refer you to the book *First Principles and First Values*, co-authored by Marc Gafni, Zak Stein, and Ken Wilber, under the name David J. Temple. David J. Temple is a pseudonym created for enabling ongoing collaborative authorship at the Center for World Philosophy and Religion. The two primary authors behind David J. Temple are Marc Gafni and Zak Stein, and for different projects, specific writers will be named as part of the collaboration, such as Ken Wilber and others.

Three other volumes complete this introduction: *A Return to Eros*, by Marc Gafni and Kristina Kincaid; *Your Unique Self*, by Marc Gafni; and *Education in a Time between Worlds*, by Zak Stein.

We hope that the Oral Essays in this volume, with their informal style of transmission, will serve as an allurement and entryway for you into the more formal books of the Great Library that provide the robust intellectual underpinnings of the new Story of Value.

A NOTE ABOUT THE EDITORS

This Oral Essays collection has been edited by students of the new Story of CosmoErotic Humanism. Each of us has actively participated in *One Mountain, Many Paths*, and most of us have been in deep "Holy of Holies" study with Dr. Marc Gafni for many years.

We have been privileged to find ourselves well-versed in the teachings, and even emerging as lineage-holders of CosmoErotic Humanism.[3]

We view this editing project as a privilege and a deep practice of study and clarification. We experience ourselves as a *mystical editing society*, frequently meeting and conversing together about the content—the depth of knowledge and wisdom offered here—as well as the technical intricacies involved with publishing a beautiful and coherent series of books. In so doing, we function as a "Unique Self Symphony," which itself is a Dharmic

---

3 CosmoErotic Humanism is a world philosophical movement aimed at reconstructing the collapse of value at the core of global culture. Much like Romanticism or Existentialism, CosmoErotic Humanism is not merely a theory but a movement that changes the very mood of Reality. It is an invitation to participate in evolving the source code of consciousness and culture towards a cosmocentric *ethos* for a planetary civilization.

The term CosmoErotic Humanism, initially coined by Dr. Gafni and colleagues, points to a complex, multi-faceted, layered, and nuanced evolutionary set of insights that has evolved over decades of intensive research, teaching, and spiritual practice from deep within a wide range of wisdom traditions (including the Wisdom of Solomon lineage tradition, Bodhisattva Buddhism, and Kashmir Shaivism), as well as multiple disciplines including complexity theory, chaos theory, emergence theory, molecular biology, and the more classical disciplines of the humanities.

The seeds of CosmoErotic Humanism were planted with Dr. Marc Gafni's work on a two-volume, 1,000-page opus called *Radical Kabbalah* (Integral Publishers, 2012). This scholarly work, sourced from deep study within the esoteric lineage texts of the Wisdom of Solomon, points to a non-dual, or acosmic, realization which—unlike the prevailing conceptualization of non-duality—does not efface the human being; rather, it is highly humanistic in its nature. The next step in the evolution of CosmoErotic Humanism was the insight that all of Reality is evolving Eros, which lives in, as, and through the human being.

A failure of Eros leads inexorably to the creation of narratives of "pseudo-eros." CosmoErotic Humanism is a response to the modern mental and social breakdown sourced in the proliferation of multiple forms of pseudo-eros and its broken narratives, such as rivalrous conflict governed by win/lose metrics and the dogmatic denial of intrinsic value in Cosmos, which together generate our current "global intimacy disorder."

term that connotes an omni-considerate collaboration between realized Unique Selves synergizing our unique gifts into a new emergence greater than the sum of the parts. Even as we worked diligently to standardize our editing styles, meeting on a weekly basis to debate the nuances of phrasing, we also operated from within a deep appreciation of the unique style that each editor brought to his or her work. As such, the reader might notice some variation in editing style among the books.

Please note that Dr. Marc Gafni has not reviewed these edited Oral Essays, as he is deeply engaged in writing the formal books of the Great Library. But he has been generous in responding to questions and providing overall guidance in the project. Overall, as Marc's students and students of the Dharma, we have made it a key project at the Center to publish these pieces of work relatively independently.

OUR UNIQUE ORAL-ESSAY EDITING STYLE PRESERVES THE ENERGY OF THE ORIGINAL TRANSMISSION

Dr. Marc Gafni is a uniquely gifted teacher whose oral transmission is imbued with a quality that has proven transformative for his students. Many of us feel mystically transformed by both the content and the underlying energy of the transmission style. Therefore, as we like to say, *trust the magic ways the Dharma comes through your unique understanding!*

As Marc's empowered students, colleagues, and beloved friends, we have a deep knowing that these teachings are vital for the survival and thriving of humanity as we know it, and we recognize the importance of publishing his teachings in a written format that will be accessible by future generations. At the same time, we sought to preserve the Eros of the original oral transmission with all of its nuance, power, and depth. Our intention in the editing process, to the greatest extent possible, has been to keep these spoken artifacts intact in order to maintain the flow of the original transmission. We have therefore chosen not to engage in intensive formal editing, as we found that doing so resulted in the loss of the energetic transmission that is so key to fully receiving the Dharma.

After experimenting with many ways to present these texts, we developed a specific way of laying out the text on the page. Marc, in collaboration with Zak Stein and Russian intellectual/artist Elena Maslova-Levin—and ultimately all of the editors, through many conversations—developed a unique, artistic presentation of the text, using bolding, italics, bullet points, and other stylistic features which together serve to accentuate the immediacy of the oral transmission.

As part of this editing style, intended to preserve the integrity of the original transmission, we have refrained from removing the frequent recapitulations of key themes. We found that each recapitulation contributes something vital to the rhythm and music beneath the words, like the beating drum of our hearts. These recapitulations not only review previous material but also add important new emphases, perspectives, and elements of the new Story of Value. We ask for your patience as a reader to trust the rhythm of these texts, and we trust you as a reader to have the depth and steadiness to find your way through.

KEY COMPONENTS: LINK TO THE ORIGINAL BROADCAST, EVOLUTIONARY LOVE CODES AND PRAYER

To supplement the written word, each episode includes a QR code linking to the original broadcast on YouTube, as well as occasional links to featured songs and video clips.

Each episode also centers around an "Evolutionary Love Code," formulated by Marc. These codes are part of the ongoing articulation and distillation of the Dharma as it unfolds and emerges, week by week, over the course of many years, through the mystical process we call Outrageous Love or Evolutionary Love.

Another core component of the *One Mountain, Many Paths* episodes is what Marc and Barbara called "Evolutionary Prayer." Prayer is experienced in *One Mountain* not in the old fundamentalist sense of a "cosmic vending-machine god" who is alienated from Cosmos. Marc refers to this as the "god you do not and should not believe in"—and he often adds, "the god you don't believe in does not exist."

GOD IS THE INFINITE INTIMATE

In fact, in the Dharma of CosmoErotic Humanism, a new name for God has emerged: the "Infinite Intimate," who appears in first-, second-, and third-person expressions. Marc first shared this name as he heard it whispered in 2023, although earlier intimations and formulations of the name appeared as early as 2010.

In first person, God is infinitely alive and as intimate as our own first-person experience.

In second person, God is the infinitely intimate Personhood of Cosmos that knows our name and holds us—the God about whom we say, *whenever we fall, we fall into Her hands*. This is the God who is our Beloved, Father, Mother, Lover, and Evolutionary Partner.

Finally, in third person, God inheres in all of the First Principles and First Values of Cosmos, and in the laws of science (both interior and exterior) that govern manifest Reality.

Therefore, we have a realization of God as not only the Infinity of Power but also the Infinity of Intimacy.

In *One Mountain, Many Paths*, we are reclaiming prayer at a higher level of consciousness. And we are reclaiming prayer as deep, alive, loving, and intimate conversations with God as the Infinite Intimate who knows our name.

EDITORIAL NOTE

REFLECTING ON THE CO-CREATION BETWEEN DR. MARC GAFNI AND BARBARA MARX HUBBARD

Barbara and Marc met five years before Barbara passed. As Barbara said so often, "before I met Marc, I was sure that I was done." Barbara had taught so beautifully for decades, focusing particularly on a powerful articulation of "conscious evolution." Indeed, it would not be inaccurate to say that Barbara was the greatest storyteller of conscious evolution of her time.

Conscious evolution was also a premise in Marc's thinking, but drawn from an entirely different set of sources and experiences. Barbara drew from the classical sources of evolutionary spirituality, such as Teilhard de Chardin, Buckminster Fuller, and many others.

Indeed, she was closely associated with Fuller, and was perhaps de Chardin's most ardent intellectual devotee.

Marc drew a somewhat different vision of conscious evolution from the interior sciences of the great wisdom traditions, with a primary emphasis on what he refers to as the "Solomon lineages," merged together with careful readings of the leading edges of the sciences.

In the old version of conscious evolution, the movement from unconscious to conscious was a movement of evolution by chance to evolution by choice.

Together Marc and Barbara evolved the old version of Conscious Evolution, pointing out that evolution itself was always in some sense conscious, but as Marc formulated it, the awakening to conscious evolution refers to the awakening of evolution as human consciousness, coupled with the human realization of being conscious evolution in person, and the human capacity to locate oneself within the context of the larger evolutionary story.

Marc focused his attention on an entirely different dimension of Reality, which he and his colleagues began to call CosmoErotic Humanism. The Intimate Universe, Homo amor, Unique Self and Unique Self Symphonies, God as the Infinity of Intimacy, Eros and the CosmoErotic Universe, distinctions like Role Mate, Soul Mate and Whole Mate, the Four Selves, Evolutionary Love, Outrageous Love, Evolution: the Love Story of the Universe, First Principles and First Values, Evolving Perennialism, the Evolution of Love, and many more are terms articulated by Gafni and shared with Barbara in their conversation, study, and creative engagement.

Some terms they coined together, for example "a Planetary Awakening in Love through Unique Self Symphonies," where Gafni described Unique Self Symphonies, and Barbara aligned her vision of a planetary Pentecost to Marc's vision of Unique Self Symphonies.

Other key terms were unique and articulated by Barbara, for example: conscious evolution, teleros, telerotic, from joining genes to joining genius, regenopause, vocational arousal, birthing of humanity, synergy engine, and of course her work around what she called the Wheel of Co-creation.

Ultimately, Marc and Barbara attempted to synergize their work in what they called the Wheel of Co-creation 2.0. Barbara and Marc experienced themselves as merging their respective Dharma into what they began to refer to as Conscious Evolution 2.0, or later, CosmoErotic Humanism.

The first 129 episodes of One Mountain, Many Paths took place in the last period of Barbara's life and reflect the depth and texture of the stunning evolutionary whole-mate meeting between her and Marc. As Barbara was deep in study with Marc, a lot of what she shared in Evolutionary Church was the Dharma of their deep study and collaboration.

Although sometimes it may be clear who is speaking, we generally publish these early episodes in what we are calling "one voice."

The first 129 episodes, with Marc and Barbara together, have been grouped chronologically. Episodes 130 to 400 and onwards, which were transmitted by Marc, have been grouped by topic.

THE INVITATION

We invite you to find your way into this revolution. Each one of our Unique Selves and unique gifts are desperately needed as we co-create this new Story of Value together, as part of the covenant between generations, for the sake of the whole.

Let's *play a larger game* and evolve the very source code of consciousness and culture together.

With mad love,

The Editors

LOVE OR DIE

LOCATING OURSELVES: ARTICULATING THE ESSENTIAL CONTEXT FOR THE ONE MOUNTAIN, MANY PATHS ORAL ESSAYS

SETTING OUR INTENTION

Intention setting is everything.

We're here—as da Vinci was with his cohort in the Renaissance—**to play a larger game, to participate in the evolution of love, which is to tell the new Story of Value rooted in First Principles and First Values.**

- Our intention is to recognize the critical historical juncture in which we find ourselves.
- Our intention is to take our seat at the table of history and to say, *we take responsibility for this.*
- Our intention is to participate as revolutionaries for the sake of the whole.

What we're here to do is revolution; revolution for the sake of the evolution of love.

It's a revolution for the sake of the trillions of unborn lives that will not manifest:

- The unborn loves
- The unborn creativity
- The unborn goodness
- The unborn truth
- The unborn beauty

All of it looks to us.

Not because we're engaged in grandiosity. Not at all!

- We're trembling before She.
- We're trembling with joy at the privilege.
- We're trembling with joy at the responsibility.
- We're trembling with joy at the Possibility of Possibility.
- We have to enact a new Story in this moment of time. Because it is only a new Story that can change the vector of history.

The most revolutionary act that we can do—the greatest moral imperative of this time—**is to articulate a new Story at this time between worlds and this time between stories.**

Story is not made up, as postmodernity suggests. **We all live in inescapable frameworks; our framework is the story we live in.** Right now, Reality lives according to win/lose metrics, a story that is generating existential risk. **We need to change that story.**

When we change that story, when we tell a new Story—not a made-up story, but a new Story of Value, rooted in First Principles and First Values—**then it all changes.**

We need to participate in the evolution of the source code of consciousness and culture, which is the evolution of love.

It's the most important, exciting, evolutionary, revolutionary act that we can do to alleviate suffering: to be lovers.

Like Rumi, the great poet of Sufism, we have to be "mad lovers," because it's the only sanity.

To be mad lovers is to see around the corner, to not be so obsessed with the details of the contractions of my life.

Let me see bigger.

Let me take complete care of myself in every possible way, let me completely attend to those in my circle of intimacy and influence, and then—*let me expand my circle.*

That's what we're here for.

- Our intention is to participate in the *LoveForce*, the *LoveIntelligence*, the *LoveBeauty*, the *LoveDesire* that literally animates Cosmos all the way up and all the way down.
- Our intention is to participate in the evolution of love.

[In the next few pages we will cover some key concepts which are essential to locating ourselves and setting the context for all the One Mountain, Many Paths Oral Essays. —Eds.]

OVERVIEW: EROS IS NO LONGER A LUXURY—IT'S LOVE OR DIE

Eros is life.

The failure of Eros destroys life.

Our lack of Eros is poised to destroy the world.

All civilizations have fallen because the stories that they lived in were, in some sense, stories based on rivalrous conflict governed by win/lose metrics. Every civilization was weakened by interior polarization caused by the lack of a shared Story of Value.

We now have a global civilization, but we haven't created a shared Story of Value.

We haven't solved the generator functions that caused all civilizations to fall. Our global civilization has exponential technologies and extraction models depleting the Earth of resources that took billions of years to create, which is going to lead to a civilizational collapse.

Existential risk is risk to our very existence.

The choice is clear: love or die.

It's that simple.

Eros is no longer a luxury. It is an absolute necessity for the survival of the individual and the planet.

In the last half a century, modern psychology has documented an age-old truth: a fully nourished baby who is not held in loving arms will die.

So too, our world, both personal and global—even with all the resources of intelligence and technology at our disposal—will die without being held in love, in the embrace of Eros.

We must embrace a personal path of love and a global politics of love.

Not ordinary love. Not love which is "mere human sentiment," but Eros, or what we sometimes call Outrageous Love, which is the heart of existence itself.

We live in a world of outrageous pain.

The only response is Outrageous Love.

WHAT IS EROS?

Eros is the experience of radical aliveness, moving towards, seeking, desiring ever-deeper contact and ever-greater wholeness.[4] Eros is the core fabric of Reality's being and the motivational architecture of Reality's becoming.

Eros is what animates the evolutionary impulse itself, from the very inception of Cosmos all the way to our very selves, who awaken to the realization that the evolutionary impulse throbs uniquely in each of us.

The realization of human awakening and transformation that lies at the core of the interior sciences is the invitation—or even the urgent and desperate demand—of a madly loving Cosmos animated by infinities of power and infinities of intimacy.

The demand—the desperate invitation, the plea, the tender and fierce command of Cosmos that lives inside every human being—is to awaken: to awaken to our true nature as unique incarnations of Eros and Ethos that are needed and desperately desired by All-That-Is. Said slightly differently: Reality is Eros. Or: God is Eros.

The failure of Eros destroys life. The collapse of Eros is always the hidden (or not so hidden) root cause for the collapse of ethics.

This is true both personally and collectively. We live in a moment of a worldwide and personal collapse of Eros. Our lack of Eros is poised to destroy

---

4 We define Eros through what we refer to as the Eros equation (one of a series of what we call interior science equations):

Eros = Radical Aliveness x Desiring (Growing + Seeking) x Deeper Contact x Greater Wholeness x Self Actualization/Self Transcendence (Creation [Destruction])

There are good reasons for the formal language of the interior science equations in these writings, and the reader is invited to explore them on their own, in particular, in our work, David J. Temple, *First Principles and First Values: Forty-Two Propositions on CosmoErotic Humanism, the Meta-Crisis, and the World to Come* (World Philosophy and Religion, 2024).

the world. Humanity is currently experiencing what has come to be known as existential risk, a risk to our very existence, or what I will refer to as the Second Shock of Existence.

EXISTENTIAL RISK: THE SECOND SHOCK OF EXISTENCE

The first shock of existence is the death of the human being—the realization that we will die, which dawns in human consciousness at the beginning of history. We are not talking about the biological fact of death but the *existential* realization of death. Although the interior sciences disclose that death is a portal between two days (there is vast empirical,[5] philosophical,[6] and anthro-ontological evidence[7] for the continuity of consciousness[8]), death is also, in our own direct surface experience, a stark end. And that is obviously not a bug, but a feature in the system.

---

[5] We refer to evidence gathered by the most serious of researchers, beginning with Henry and Edith Sedgwick at Cambridge University and William James at Harvard University, and continuing in highly rigorous form for the last 150 years, as recapitulated by Whiteheadian scholar David Ray Griffin in multiple volumes. See also, for example, Dean Radin, *Real Magic: Unlocking Your Natural Psychic Abilities to Create Everyday Miracles* (Potter/TenSpeed/Harmony, 2018), *The Conscious Universe: The Scientific Truth of Psychic Phenomena* (HarperCollins, 2010), and other books. Or see the earlier classic by Frederic William Henry Myers, *Human Personality and Its Survival of Bodily Death* (Longmans, Green, 1907).

[6] This requires a cogent analysis of materialism and dualism, and the introduction of the far more cogent third possibility, which we have called "pan-interiority."

[7] We discuss Anthro-Ontology in some depth in *First Principles and First Values*, and see also the fuller conversation in David J. Temple, *First Principles and First Values: Towards an Evolving Perennialism: Introducing the Anthro-Ontological Method*—both published by World Philosophy and Religion Press, in conjunction with Integral Publishers. For now, we will simply define it as an "innate and clear interior gnosis directly available to the human being."

[8] See Dr. Marc Gafni and Dr. Zachary Stein's essay in preparation, "Beyond Death: Anthro-Ontology, Philosophy, and Empiricism." This essay is slated to appear in the book *Towards a World Religion: Homo Amor Essays*. The essay is also the ground for a larger book by the same authors, *Twelve Portals to Life Beyond Death: Responding to the Second Shock of Existence,* in which we discuss three forms of material: the empirical, the philosophical, and the anthro-ontological, and show how each form discredits the notion of death as the end.

Our first-person experience is that death ends this life. It is not the *totality* of our experience if we go deeper inside, but it is obviously intended to be the central, potent, and painful dimension of every human life. Indeed, as Ernest Becker potently reminded us, the denial of death is at our peril.

All the stories and all the plotlines and all the threads of living end at that moment. Whatever happens beyond, we have an actual experience of ending. **Paradoxically, that ending, the experience of the finality of mortality, is what presses us into life.** From the implicit demand of the first shock of existence, human beings were activated and pressed into creative emergence, and what emerged was all of human culture, both interior and exterior.

The second shock of existence is the realization of the potential death of all humanity. After all the stages of human history—matter, life, and mind in all of their stages of evolutionary unfolding—we have come to this place in the evolution of humanity, in which the gap between our exponentially expanding exterior technologies and our stalled (or even regressing) interior technologies of value has created dire catastrophic and existential risks.

This gap generates extraction models and exponential growth curves, rivalrous conflicts based on win/lose metrics, tragedies of the commons, and multipolar traps, in which everyone has to keep producing to the nth degree, including weaponized exponential threats to our very existence because we are afraid that the other parties are going to do it and not be transparent—hide it from us and then dominate us.

GENERATOR FUNCTIONS FOR EXISTENTIAL RISK

Let's outline clearly the main *generator functions for existential risk*.

Rivalrous conflicts governed by zero-sum, win/lose metrics. Rivalrous conflicts generate extraction models at the core of the economic system and exponential growth curves. Both of these drive and are driven by a contrived system of artificially manufactured desires and needs, delivered into culture by ever more precise forms of micro-targeting to individuals and groups through the ever more immersive environment of the internet.

Next, rivalrous conflicts and exponential growth curves animated by win/lose metrics generate **complicated, fragile world systems** highly vulnerable to myriad forms of collapse. Fragile local systems are made exponentially more fragile on a global level by our inability to meet global challenges with social, legal, political, economic, and ethical infrastructures that remain largely local.

All of this is a direct result of the failure to develop more adequate interior technologies that would be sufficiently compelling to displace "rivalrous conflict governed by win/lose metrics" as the motivational architecture for the human life world.

This failure has led to the conditions that will cause the implosion of systems that are already and quite literally on the brink of collapsing themselves. That's what we mean by the *second shock of existence*.

To recapitulate: the second shock of existence is not the death of the human being, but the potential death of humanity.

It is the *Death Star* moment of our species.

THE DECONSTRUCTION OF INTRINSIC VALUE

We stand in this moment poised between utopia and dystopia, at a time between worlds and a time between stories. We need a new Story of Value, eternal yet evolving, rooted in First Principles and First Values, which would become a universal grammar of value and a context for our diversity.

This is exactly what the Renaissance was. It was a time between worlds and a time between stories. In the Renaissance, we had recently been challenged by the Black Death, a pandemic that swept across Europe. The Black Death destroyed between a third to half of Europe and a huge part of

Asia. People died horrifically, brutally, in the streets. They had no idea how to meet this challenge, and so, in response to the Black Death, da Vinci and Ficino and their cohorts understood that they had to tell a new Story of Value.

That story was the story of modernity. Did they get it right?

- They got part of it right, which birthed, to use Jürgen Habermas' phrase, "the dignities of modernity," such as new ways of gathering information and universal human rights.
- But they also deconstructed the source of Value. They lost the basis for the Good, the True, and the Beautiful.

The basis used to be divine revelation: *God told us*. But this claim was owned by religion, and every religion began to overreach and over-claim. The revelation was thus often mediated through cultural categories and wasn't fully accurate.

Modernity threw out revelation, but was unable to establish a new basis for value.

Value was just assumed to be real. As it says in the founding document of the American Revolution: *We hold these truths to be self-evident*—that is, *we don't really have a basis for value; we just take it as a given.*

In other words, modernity took out a loan of social capital from the traditional world. The source of value was never worked out.

And then, gradually, value began to collapse.

- The Universe Story began to collapse.
- The belief that the Good, the True, and the Beautiful are real began to collapse.
- The belief that Love is real began to collapse.

As Bertrand Russell is reported to have said, "I cannot see how to refute the arguments for the subjectivity of ethical values, but I find myself incapable of believing that all that is wrong with wanton cruelty is that I do not like it."

What do you do if you grew up in a world in which value is not real? A world without a source of value, without a Universe Story, without a story of human identity, without a story of desire, without a narrative of power?

In the words of W.B. Yeats, *the center does not hold.*

- You have a collapse at the very center of society, because you no longer have Eros.
- You no longer have a Reality in which value is real, and so you have this lingering sense of emptiness.
- You have a complete collapse at the very center.
- We become *the hollow men and the stuffed men*, gesture without form.

And that's the source of our current existential risk.

THE DEEPER ROOT CAUSE OF THE META-CRISIS: A GLOBAL INTIMACY DISORDER

Above, I have outlined the major generator functions of existential risk. But there is a deeper cause for the existential risk that lurks underneath the rivalrous conflict governed by win/lose metrics and the fragile systems they engender.

And we cannot take the Death Star down without discerning and addressing this. We have already alluded to this root cause above, but at this point we need to make it more explicit so that, from this context, the adequate root response will become clear.

Modernity threw out the revelation, but was unable to establish a new basis for value.

This ostensibly surprising statement can be understood in a few simple steps:

1. All of the catastrophic and existential risk challenges we face are global: from climate change to artificial intelligence, pandemics, systems collapse, and exponential arms races.
2. Every global challenge self-evidently requires a global solution.
3. Global solutions can only be implemented with global co-ordination.
4. Global co-ordination is impossible without global coherence.
5. Global coherence is only possible if there is a global resonance between the parts.
6. Global resonance is only possible if we have global intimacy.

ONLY A SHARED STORY OF VALUE CAN GENERATE GLOBAL INTIMACY

Global intimacy—just like intimacy in a couple—is only possible when there is a shared story.

Not just a shared history, but a shared Story of Value.

- It is only a shared global story that can generate a new emergent quality of intimacy: global intimacy.
- A shared Story of Value must be rooted in shared ordinating values, or what we have called evolving First Values and First Principles.
- Intimacy requires a shared grammar of value as a matrix for a shared Story of Value.

The global intimacy disorder is the root cause for existential risk. The global intimacy disorder underlies the core generator functions for existential risk.

The global intimacy disorder is rooted in the failure to experience ourselves in a field of shared intrinsic value. This failure derives from the deconstruction of value.

Indeed, it is wholly accurate to say that **the root cause of the two generator functions of existential risk is the failed story of intrinsic value, or what we might also call the breakdown of Eros.**

1. The first generator function is **the success story.** Our modern success story is rivalrous conflict governed by win/lose metrics, which violates all the terms of the Intimacy Equation: there is no shared identity and no mutuality of recognition, feeling, value or purpose, and instead of *relative* otherness, there is *alienated* otherness. Such a story generates complicated fragile systems with no allurement or intimacy between the parts, systems which optimize for efficiency (as an expression of win/lose metrics) and not for resiliency and life.
2. The second generator function is **the deconstruction of intrinsic value** itself. The deconstruction of value is the sense that human value does not participate in the intrinsic value of the Real, for the Real is dogmatically declared to have no intrinsic value. Thus, there is no shared identity between the interior of the human being and Reality. There is no common participation in a field of shared intrinsic value. Instead of being intimate with value, we are alienated from value. And only intrinsic value can arouse will: political, moral, and social will.

To sum up, without a shared grammar of value there is no global intimacy, and therefore no global coherence, and no global coordination in response to catastrophic and existential risk, which means, put simply, there will be, quite literally, no future.

HEALING THE GLOBAL INTIMACY DISORDER REQUIRES THE EVOLUTION OF INTIMACY

But we are not hopeless. On the contrary, we are filled with great hope. Hope is a memory of the future. That memory of the future *is* the direct hit that takes down the Death Star, the culture of death. **The direct hit must be**—as it has always been in history—**the emergence of a new stage of evolution.**

Crisis is an evolutionary driver, and every crisis is, at its core, a crisis of intimacy: from the oxygen crisis of the single cells dying which generated multicellular life at the dawn of existence, to the existential risk in this very moment.[9]

The direct hit is therefore structurally self-evident: the evolution of intimacy itself.

What is intimacy, as a structure of Cosmos all the way down and all the way up the evolutionary chain? We engage this inquiry in depth in other writings, but for now we will simply adduce what we have called the "Intimacy Equation":

> *Intimacy = shared identity in the context of [relative] otherness* x *mutuality of recognition* x *mutuality of pathos* x *mutuality of value* x *mutuality of purpose*

Intimacy is about the capacity of parts to generate a *shared identity* while retaining their otherness, or distinct identity. This requires multiple mutualities, including recognition, pathos (or feeling), value, and purpose. The parts must recognize and feel each other, even as they share value and purpose. But all of this must lead to intimate union—and not pathological

---

9 We demonstrate this principle in some depth in the multi-volume series, *The Universe: A Love Story* (forthcoming) (https://worldphilosophyandreligion.org/early-ontologies), *The Intimate Universe: Global Intimacy Disorder as Cause for Global Action Paralysis* (forthcoming), and in other writings of CosmoErotic Humanism.

fusion, where the distinct identity of the parts disappears—like subatomic particles that successfully become an atom, or two people who successfully become a couple.

THE DECONSTRUCTION OF VALUE IS THE DECONSTRUCTION OF INTIMACY

We have identified the global intimacy disorder as the root cause of existential risk. But the underlying ultimate failure of intimacy is the deconstruction of value itself.

The deconstruction of value means that human value does not participate in any sense of intrinsic value of the Real. This is not about individual *values*, but about *the Field of Value* that underlies all of them. **When the human being**—moved, often sincerely or even nobly, by myriad cultural, historical, and psychological confusions—**claims to have stepped out of the Field of Value, then intimacy itself is deconstructed.**

The deconstruction of value is the deconstruction of intimacy.

In the absence of a shared Story of Value, a story that is an authentic expression of Reality's Eros, a story rooted in *pseudo-Eros* takes center stage and becomes the generator function for existential risk. Our modern pseudo-Eros story is *rivalrous conflict governed by win/lose metrics*. Such a story catalyzes in its wake the second generator function of existential risk: *complicated fragile systems with no allurement or intimacy between the parts*. It is in that sense that we have argued that the first generator function for existential risk is the success story.

- The failure of intimacy is precisely the impotent experience that there is no shared identity between the interior of the human being and Reality. **There is no shared identity in the sense of any kind of common participation in a field of shared intrinsic value.**
- **But only a shared Story of Value can arouse the global will**

required to engage catastrophic and existential risk. For it is only global political, moral, and social will—and we can even say *erotic* will—that can generate the most Good, True and Beautiful world that we have always known is possible.

THE EVOLUTION OF LOVE IS THE TELLING OF A NEW STORY

Coupled with the Intimacy Equation is the scientifically grounded realization, in both the exterior and interior sciences, that Reality is a progressive deepening of intimacies, or, said slightly differently:

Reality is Evolution. Evolution is the evolution of intimacy.

- The evolution of intimacy requires—both personally and collectively—a deeper, more accurate discernment of the nature of our universe, ourselves, and our beloveds.
- This new discernment generates a new global Story of Value.
- The new global Story of Value generates an emergent, heretofore unseen global intimacy and heals the global intimacy disorder.

The new Story of Value is the direct hit that takes down the Death Star and replaces it with the hope that invokes the memory of our best future.

Global intimacy facilitates global coherence, which facilitates global coordination, which activates the possibility of our creative and effectively coordinated global responses to the global meta-crisis in its entirety and its specific expressions.

To solve Bertrand Russell's challenge—the apparent argument for the subjectivity of ethical values—**we have to reground value theory in eternal yet evolving First Principles and First Values, and articulate a new Story of Value.**

This is what we call CosmoErotic Humanism.

CosmoErotic Humanism—together with other emergent strands—**needs to become the ground of a world religion as a context for our diversity**. We need religion, even as we need science, to articulate a shared global grammar of value.

As we said at the beginning, our choice is simple: love or die.

- To love means to participate in the evolution of love, which is the evolution of the human Story of Value.
- To love means to evolve and activate a new cultural enlightenment—rooted in a new narrative of identity, a new narrative of value, a new narrative of intimate communion, a new narrative of desire, a new narrative of power—all of which will birth new narratives of economics and politics.
- The evolution of love is the telling of a new Story.

The new Story that must be told is a love story, for in fact that is the deepest truth of Reality, rooted in the best exterior and interior sciences, that we have at this moment in time:

- Reality is not merely a fact. Reality is a story.
- Reality is not an ordinary story. Reality is a love story.
- Reality is not an ordinary love story. Reality is an Outrageous Love Story.

Story doesn't mean it's *made-up*.

It means doing the hard work of integrating the validated insights of the traditional world, the modern world, and the postmodern world.

This is the intention at the heart of telling the new Story of CosmoErotic Humanism.

ABOUT THIS VOLUME

In a time between devolution and evolution, between destruction and creation, the response that is needed is a new story. This book is a sacred call to step into your evolutionary purpose, to join with others in synergistic action, and to co-create a world infused with Evolutionary Love.

This book weaves together timeless wisdom, evolutionary spirituality, and radical intimacy to ignite a planetary awakening. Through meditations, deeply moving prayers, transformative teachings, and a vision for humanity's next step, this book guides you on a journey beyond the separations of ego into the fullness of your Unique Self.

Each chapter offers a powerful transmission of evolutionary wisdom, revealing the patterns of love, creativity, and transformation encoded in the fabric of Reality. It opens with a meditation on the evolutionary impulse, calling readers to awaken to the deep intelligence guiding the Cosmos. Then, we explore the transformation of love from ego-driven desire into an awakened force of connection and healing.

Each of us carries a distinct, irreplaceable essence meant to be given as a gift to the world. In this book, you are guided through the process of identifying and activating your Unique Self, the core expression of your evolutionary potential. You are meant to live as a fully embodied expression of divine love in motion, and that ecstatic energy leads to co-creation.

This book also presents a radical reframing of personal struggle and wounding as part of a larger evolutionary process. Our deepest pain can be transformed into a source of our greatness, and life's challenges are not obstacles, but invitations to greater wholeness.

At the heart of this teaching is the vision of the Unique Self Symphony—a new social, spiritual, and evolutionary framework where each individual's gifts, when fully expressed, contribute alongside others' unique gifts to impact evolutionary transformations in the whole. This is explored through the study of evolutionary spirituality, deep introspection, and the self-organizing intelligence of the Cosmos.

The Universe is not random and meaningless; it is a love story, calling you to participate in its unfolding. Your uniqueness is not a mark of separation but the key to deep connection and co-creation. Evolution itself is Love in Action, and your personal love story is chapter and verse in this evolutionary love story. The crises of our time are not signs of breakdown but the birth pains of a new humanity, inviting us to rise together in a global symphony of transformation.

With poetic depth and prophetic vision, this book invites you to step beyond ordinary love into the ecstatic urgency of Evolutionary Love. You are not an extra on the set of Reality. You are needed. Your gifts, your voice, your love—all are essential for the awakening of humanity.

Are you ready to embrace your divine calling and play your unique note in the Unique Self Symphony?

Volume 3

These oral essays are lightly edited talks delivered by Marc Gafni and Barbara Marx Hubbard between March and May 2017.

CHAPTER ONE

STEPPING INTO A MIGHTY EVOLUTIONARY JOURNEY

Episode 21 — March 18, 2017

MEDITATION ON THE EVOLUTIONARY IMPULSE WITHIN

We are on a mighty evolutionary journey together. We are right at the moment of an awakening of an entire planetary body—either to devolution and destruction or to evolution and creation.

These teachings come to you at *that* precise moment of evolution.

Take a moment to put your attention on the mind of God. Go back to the origin of creation and experience the spiral of the evolutionary impulse, through billions and billions of years, from:

- The universe
- To earth
- To life
- To animal life
- To human life
- And now, to you

It's coming through the impulse of your being, from the lowest chakra, all the way up through your heart. Take that impulse of evolution in your heart right now. Feel it there—the mighty impulse awakening your heart in love.

Now imagine a time on Earth when all of the world is paying attention like they did during the millennium or the lunar landing. Everyone is paying attention to the Unique Self Symphony, celebrating the birth of a new humanity.

Now, feel that impulse of the Divine, the God force within you, going up through you and out through the top of your head, into the noosphere or the thinking layer of Earth.

Take a moment to simply feel your unique expression as a component of the Unique Self Symphony. **Whatever it is that God gave you to express as your very best, as your greatest self, give it to this noosphere, this church. This is your statement for today in the Book of Life.**

The universal symphony, the Unique Self Symphony, is orchestrated by the divine process of creation.

It's the interior of evolution inside you that is coded with the evolutionary impulse.

Let your breath go up and down. Activate your own unique expression within the Unique Self Symphony. We are aligned in love, moving forward toward our collective awakening as *Homo universalis,* born into our god-like powers to co-evolve with nature and to co-create with Spirit.

WE PRAY TO THE INFINITY OF INTIMACY

We are in Bethlehem. We are founding a new movement together that emerges out of the space between us—the space of love, the space of Evolutionary Love, the space of Outrageous Love that is the Unique Self Symphony.

We are laying down the framework, laying down the tracks, the groundwork for this to spread around the world. A deep bow to every single person who opens the space in the heart.

We come with the notion of being committed to building a resonant space.

Episcopalian churches are pretty empty.

Fundamentalist churches are pretty full—that is a tragedy!

In the liberal world, we do not come to church, except occasionally when we want a little entertainment.

Whenever I want to hear the Spirit of God moving alive, I go to a Black Gospel, African American, Fundamentalist church. Do I agree with their dogma? I do not. Do I agree with lots of their politics? I do not, but the Spirit of God is moving there. The Spirit of God is moving because they get it, though they may not have the language that the god you don't believe in doesn't exist.

God is not merely, as the old religions told us, the Infinity of Power:

- God is the Infinity of Intimacy
- God is the God that Rumi talked about when he said, *Every place I fall, I fall into God's hands.*
- God is the Beloved who catches us no matter what and where.
- God is the personal face of the Intimate Universe.
- God is the God whom Solomon talked about.

This is the God spoken of by the great Solomon, when he said, *smolo tachat l'roshi v'yemino techabkeni*[1]—God's left hand is beneath my head, His right arm is embracing me, *tocho ratzuf b'ahava* the insides are lined with love.[2]

---

1 Song of Solomon 2:6.
2 Song of Solomon 3:10.

THE HOLY AND THE BROKEN *HALLELUJAH*

As we move into prayers, we move into the place in which we offer *the holy and the broken Hallelujah*.

Why do we keep doing the same thing again? In a world without depth, where we want to be entertained, we try and shake it up, do it differently every single time to get entertained.

When we are laying down the tracks for a new religion, we want to go deep.

To go deep, you do it again and again.

How many people have ever said, *I love you*? We have all said, *I love you*.

How many people have ever had sex? Here is the big question. How many people have had sex twice? Really, you already did that! You kept doing the same thing, week after week. *Are you for real? What were you thinking? You did that already!* Why do you repeat something? Why do you say, *I love you* again?

I say again, *I love you*. I make love *again*—whether in spirit, in body, in emotion, in heart—because I want to go deeper. I am not looking for just a new body or a new person to say it to. **I want to go deeper and deeper and deeper, saying, *I love you*, to my entire circle of intimacy and influence.**

We reclaim the evolutionary God, and as we reclaim evolutionary prayer, we liberate prayer from its fundamentalist hold and offer it up. Here is the *pointing-out instruction*.

POINTING-OUT INSTRUCTION FOR PRAYER

Can you hear me talking? *Yes, you can.*

I can hear you talking. I heard Barbara talking. How did I hear Barbara talking? Using my ears.

But, it was not just my physical ears. I was using my intelligence. My intelligence heard Barbara talking.

This is a Tibetan Buddhist practice called a pointing-out instruction. We point out what prayer means.

When I, with my intelligence, heard Barbara talking, am I the most intelligent person in the State of California? I don't think so! I am not all of the intelligence in California. There is a lot of intelligence.

Am I separate from the Source of Intelligence?

No! I am part of the larger Field of Intelligence. There is not just Gafni's intelligence.

My intelligence participates in the larger Field of Reality.

If my intelligence could hear Barbara speaking, could it be that when Barbara prays, the intelligence of all of Reality can't hear her speaking? Of course not! Of course not!

When we pray, the Infinity of Intimacy, the Field of LoveIntelligence of all of Reality, hears and holds and kisses and loves every word we say.

We offer up our *holy and broken Hallelujah*. Every place we fall, we fall into God's hands. We go in, and we offer up. We sing with, and we sing along. We write down the note we want to say to ourselves, that we want to offer as our prayer. We go into and literally feel God!

The god we don't believe in doesn't exist.

The Infinity of Intimacy knows our name, hears every word of this hymn, and every word of the prayer we're about to offer.

When we pray, we open all the gates. We align with the intimacy of Reality and say, *Help me! Hold me! Mother! Amen!*

Let us feel it! Let us pray like we do every week, the holy and the broken *Hallelujah*!

PRAYERS TO THE INFINITY OF INTIMACY

We affirm the dignity of personal need, and we realize that we live in a world of outrageous pain. The only response to outrageous pain is Outrageous Love.

Outrageous Love means:

> that everything matters,
> that every person matters,
> that all our pain matters,
> that all our angst matters,
> that every moment of brokenness matters,
> and that we are never alone.

We pray before God. The god we don't believe in doesn't exist. We pray and offer our prayers to the Infinity of Intimacy, for ourselves, for our friends.

The gates are open now! When the gates are open, there is grace. When I pray to a *place of grace*, Reality—literally God—hears.

Can you imagine God sitting before us? The Infinity of Power sitting in a chair, the second face of God, and you say, *I'm busy. Sorry, I'm busy. I can't make the effort God, sorry! I was a little busy. I was just doing something else.*

My life, who cares? Oh my God! Do you get it, my friends?

The fundamentalists got a few things wrong in the dogma, but they got some things right in the Infinity of Intimacy.

For us to have an evolutionary family, to invoke a Unique Self Symphony, we need to know that our prayers matter.

We can offer our prayers.

We are not *extra* on the set.

We are not entertainment.

We are raising up and offering our prayers. That is the good news of Reality.

The good news of Reality is that no one is alone.

The good news of Reality is that the same God, in the third person, which is the infinite laws of physics, the laws of chemistry, and the laws of all of the Infinite Power of Reality, all of that third face of God is sitting on this chair with us, loving each of us open, knowing our names, and offering it up.

So, it is good, and the word is good.

We're an evolutionary family.

We're the Evolutionary Church.

We're laying down the tracks together.

We are reclaiming the knowing that God, the Infinity of Intimacy, the evolutionary impulse knows our name and holds us in every moment. The obstacles are melted away, and the word is good.

EVOLUTIONARY TESTAMENT OF CO-CREATION

I am going to reference my (Barbara's) book, *The Evolutionary Testament of Co-Creation: The Promise Will Be Kept.*

Several years ago, I asked the Universe, *What kind of person could handle all the new power of humanity (biotech, nanotech, quantum computing, artificial intelligence, and space travel)? Who is able to incarnate that as a human without destroying the world?*

I took a walk, and I saw a beautiful monastery. I saw a cross and a group of hang gliders jumping off a higher mountain, floating in butterfly wings above the cross. I had the phrase come to me, mass metamorphosis.

Then this phrase of St. Paul arrived in my head:

> *Behold, I show you a mystery.*
> *We shall not all sleep,*
> *we shall all be changed at any moment,*
> *in the twinkling of an eye,*
> *at the last trumpet, and the trumpet is sounding.*[3]

I was so thrilled. I realized that possibly the meaning of the resurrection of Jesus Christ was to reveal the possibility of the metamorphosis of humanity—a new person, a new body, a new consciousness, a new light.

With that, I checked into the Mount Calvary Monastery for a silent retreat. The next week, I picked up a Bible. I had not been a reader of the Bible. I had tried to be an Episcopalian and had failed. I come from a Jewish agnostic secular background.

As I started to read the New Testament with evolutionary eyes, I came to an epiphany about the life of Jesus. As he said: you will do the works that I do and greater works than these will you do in the fullness of time because I go to the Father.[4]

What *does* that mean? I go to the divine impulse in me, incarnated as me. I do this so that you know that you shall all be changed in a moment.

I had been a friend of the world-changing Jonas Salk, who played a pivotal role in devising and implementing a safe and effective vaccine against polio. He had taken me down to the biological laboratories in California where they were saying, *stamp out physical death!*

---

3   1 Corinthians 15:51-58.
4   John 14:12.

I had been a futurist, working with people who are studying artificial intelligence. They felt we could upload ourselves into silicon. I am not saying any of this is true or not true, but we are already attempting to do the work.

As I started to read the New Testament, I became aware that it is a coded evolutionary text. This is true of all the great scriptures of the world, but this one is particularly true because **Jesus was a future human! He is what we are becoming!**

WE ARE INSPIRING A PLANETARY PENTECOST

This is really where it all got started, The Day of Pentecost after Jesus's crucifixion, after the resurrection, after the story that Mary Magdalene was able to tell: *He is here! He is here!*

They couldn't believe her. They couldn't believe it could have happened to a woman to see first. But, she did. And seeing him after the crucifixion changed the entire world. It was not the teaching. It was not the Sermon on the Mount. It was the *reappearance.*

I am relating this to ourselves in an amazing way. Here is a brief description:

They all gather together [these are the disciples], and when the day of Pentecost was fully come, they were all with one accord in one place. Suddenly, there came a sound from heaven, as of a rushing, mighty wind, and it filled all the house where they were sitting. And there appeared unto them, cloven tongues as of fire, and it sat upon each of them.

They were totally enlivened by Spirit.

They were all filled with the Holy Ghost and began to speak in other tongues as the Spirit gave them utterance. There were Jews dwelling in Jerusalem, devout men of every nation under Heaven. When it was told that this was going on, the multitude came and were confounded because every man heard them speaking in his own language.[5]

These are all different languages in the upper room at the time of the Pentecost, and they heard it in their own language. They were amazed.

They said, *Behold, are not these who speak Galileans? How then do we each hear them in our own tongue wherein we were born?* They were all amazed and were in doubt, saying, *What meaneth this? These men are full of wine!* But Peter, standing up with the 11, lifted up his voice and said, *Ye men of Judea, and all who dwell in Jerusalem, be this known unto you: we are not drunk, seeing it is but the third hour of the morning.* But this is what was spoken of by the prophet Joel, *It shall come to pass in the last days, saith God, I will pour out my spirit upon all flesh, and your sons and your daughters shall prophesy, and your young men shall see visions, and your old men shall dream dreams.*[6]

Here is the writing that came to me after reading that:

> Now dearly beloved, your time has come. You are the second generation of disciples. You are to go forth and tell the new story to your generation. You are to tell the world: We are rising. You now have the capacity to do the works that I did and greater works can you do. You, who believe in your capacity to do as I did, are the new disciples. You will work together for the Planetary Pentecost.

Now guess what that is—it is the Unique Self Symphony—and here I described it. This was written in 1980, before I had ever known about the Unique Self Symphony.

The Planetary Pentecost is the alternative to Armageddon. It is a time on Earth when all those who choose to evolve occupy the upper room of consciousness, simultaneously. In this aligned Field of Love and expectation, you will all hear, in your own language, in your own words,

---

5 Acts 2:2-8.
6 Acts 2: 7-17.

in your own inner voices, the mighty works of God that you are to do. You will be empowered with the powers of a natural Christ.[7]

Is this true already? I'm speaking to you all over the Earth, on the internet, traveling at the speed of light.

> *You will be able to heal yourselves, to restore the Earth, to emancipate the untapped genius of all those who so believe.*

The media, your planetary nervous system, will pulse with light as it reports on the stories of your transformation.

Then, I gave this book to Marc, and I said, *Marc, is it possible that God and Christ are speaking through us now? That happened before?* He said, *Yes!* Here is what he wrote in the afterword:

You are a Unique Self who represents an irreducibly precious story of essence that is being written throughout your life. When your Unique Self awakens, you become an expression of God's will, and you are able to hear the voice of divine revelation. All of us!

When your awakened Unique Self, sensitive to the voice of God's new revelation, joins with the genius of an ancient sacred text like the Bible, then the desperately needed miracle of revelation—so critical for our time—is made manifest.

To whom does God speak?

Spirit speaks in three voices: I, We, and It. Barbara has heard the voice of God spoken in the second voice, interpreting and writing commentary on the sacred texts. She has written an Outrageous Love Letter back to God

---

[7] Barbara Marx Hubbard, *The Evolutionary Testament of Co-Creation: The Promise Will Be Kept.*

after reading God's personalized love letter to her, in the form of the sacred biblical text.

Every one of us is hearing the voice from within.

And when we speak, it amplifies its meaning.

Let it inspire every one of us. The day of Pentecost, the Unique Self Symphony, is arising.

We wanted to introduce some of the texts of the Evolutionary Church. The first major text is Barbara's wonderful *Evolutionary Testament*. It is gorgeous. I was privileged to write an afterword for it as we were getting to know each other. It is a guiding force for the Evolutionary Church.

The second text is called *Radical Kabbalah*. *Radical Kabbalah*, like *Evolutionary Testament*, is a guiding text for the Evolutionary Church.

We have Christian texts. We have Hebrew mystical texts. We have Sufi texts. But the four texts that are our guiding texts are *Evolutionary Testament* and *Conscious Evolution,* two gorgeous texts which Barbara wrote and two texts that I was privileged to write, *Radical Kabbalah* (which is two volumes) and *Your Unique Self.*

Those are the four core foundation texts.

I want to share with you a Unique Self Symphony teaching from *Radical Kabbalah,* a wild and holy and wonderful and awesome story.

Oh my god! Oh my god! Oh my god!

Here is the text—are you ready?

Some people say he is a little too excited about this!

I'm so excited! I'm so excited to be offering, together with Barbara Marx Hubbard, and to all of us together, the texts of our new church.

May there be more texts!

May we all write texts and they all join!

We have to have some anchoring texts, which articulate the beginning of this *dharma*. Barbara and I have committed our next two years, God willing! God should give us health, prosperity, dignity, and goodness to write the new texts.

We are now working on three major new texts.

A KABBALISTIC STORY OF DIVINE CALLING

Here is a story of calling, friends. What is his name? His name is Moses. Moses receives revelation, and it happens to come from the middle of a burning bush. That revelation says, *Moses, I got a job for you.*

Moses says (as people often say to burning bushes), *I am not interested. I am busy. I got a life to live!* We have a scripture on this, Exodus, Chapter 4. *God, I got a life. I got things going on! I'm running stuff. I'm running my New Age movement. I can't really listen to you. I have all these egoic disguises. God, you are awesome; I'm busy.*

And God says, *No, no. Moses, I do not think you get it. This is God talking, ehiyeh asher ehiyeh, I am that I am! This is God calling you!*

Moses says—*lo ish devarim anochi*—in the original Hebrew—I am not a man of words.

Then, Moses says, *k'vad-peh u'k'vad lashon anokh—I am a stu-stu-stu-stutterer.*

So, Moses says to God, *I stutter, I am not a man of words, I cannot do this job! Get someone who is refined, who has taken speaking courses, who knows elocution.*

And God says to Moses, *No, No, No, my friend, I want you!*

That's in the book of Exodus. This is from *Radical Kabbalah*, when we get to the fifth book of the Bible. The Bible is considered, by tradition, the word of God; whatever that means, it is the word of God. The fifth book of the Bible begins with the phrase, *eilu hadevarim*. These are the words that Moses spoke.

Now one second, let's just get this straight. It just said in Exodus that Moses says, I am not a man of *devarim*. I am not a man of words. Then three books later, Moses has gone through this transformation, and the person who wasn't a man of words now becomes the ultimate man of words.

What happened?

How did the man, who was a stutterer, the man who before the burning bush was not a man of words, who refuses the divine call to give his unique gift into the Unique Self Symphony and to rise to leadership—how does he become the man of words? What happens?

What is the transformation?

How does he become, *eilu hadevarim*—these are the words. Deuteronomy means, these are the words—*eilu hadevarim*.

Who is speaking *the* words which are *the* word of God? Moses!

How could Moses be speaking the word of God?

Isn't Moses just a human being?

Many interpretations, many mystics, say: *Well, you know, Moses becomes a channel. Moses empties himself out completely—no Moses left. Moses is a channel, and the word of God speaks through Moses.*

My friends, that could be. That is a beautiful understanding.

But, I want to share with you something even deeper, which is the deepest teaching of Evolutionary Church. This is the teaching offered in *Radical Kabbalah*. It is the teaching of the great lineage masters. The great lineage masters say: The reason the word of Moses becomes the word of God is not because Moses becomes a channel through an absence or effacement of his Moses-ness. No!

Moses has so embraced his Moses-ness, he has so embraced his Unique Self, he has so embraced the unique expression of intimacy that is Moses, that:

> *By becoming his Unique Self, by becoming his Evolutionary Unique Self, by becoming fully Moses, by finding the voice of Moses, the voice of God speaks!*

When Barbara finds the voice of Barbara, then God is alive and speaking.

What we *all* have to do:

- We've got to get out of our contraction!
- We've got to get out of our smallness!
- We've got to get over ourselves!
- We've got to give up being right!

We want to get out of the small egoic contraction, step out of our emptiness, and rise as our fullness.

We realize we are part of the seamless coat of the Universe, part of the One. We realize we are part of the seamless, though not featureless, coat of the Universe, part of the One.

Moses is a unique feature of the seamless coat of the Universe.

Moses is God's unique intimacy.

Moses is a Unique Self.

Moses is an Evolutionary Unique Self.

Once I realize I am an Evolutionary Unique Self, playing my instrument, my unique instrument, I can never give Barbara's resonance. I can never give Barbara's message. No matter what I do, I cannot inspire in the particular, unique, and gorgeous way that Barbara Marx Hubbard inspires. Therefore, I get to fall in love with Barbara. You get it? **I get to fall on my knees in devotion because I am in devotion before a unique and gorgeous Evolutionary Unique Self**—a clear, divine voice that says, *vayidabeir adonai el-mosheh leimoel mosheh leimor*, "God spoke to Moses saying…"

God spoke to Barbara saying,

God spoke to Marc saying, but not in a New Age way, not in a casual way, *We've got to do the work!*

> Moses starts in the book of Exodus as, *I am not a man of words.*
> He is contracted.
> He is confused.
> He has got to grow.
> He has got to mature.
> He has got to practice.

Like all of us:

> He has to walk through the depression.
> He has to walk through the sadness.
> There's no way around it.
> The only way is through!

And, we have got to pray. I have to always ask, *What is love?* I want to know what love is. Through the heartache and the pain, I keep screaming out to God. God, tell me what love is, and tell me how to be my Unique Self.

Tell me how to join the Unique Self Symphony.

Tell me how to give my gifts of Outrageous Love.

Not ordinary love. Not the love that is contracted and a strategy of the ego. But Barbara Marx Hubbard, as a unique expression, the Evolutionary Unique Self of Outrageous Love. Outrageous Love that can only be given by Barbara-ness.

LETTING THE EGO FLOWER INTO YOUR UNIQUE SELF

The holy text says—with this, we finish, and then we offer our prayer. We offer our prayer, but we've got to get the final text. Here it is, *shekhinatei dabrei m'pumei d'moshe.*[8]

The *Shekhinah*, the divine voice, speaks to the lips of Moses. Not because Moses has disappeared but because Moses, for the first time, has appeared.

Our invitation to ourselves, my friends, is: the Evolutionary Church is not a church led by Marc or by Barbara. It's a church which is us, Evolutionary Unique Selves joining hands in symphony, knowing that the next great Buddha is the sangha.

The sangha is made up, not of effaced, New Age disappeared selves, who pretend to be part of the One, but are harboring secret resentments and ego.

No! No! No! When you pretend to have gotten rid of ego, ego comes back and bites you—in every possible way.

No!

We have let our ego flower and mature into Unique Self. Ego points to Unique Self.

Ego is the sense that I exist, but not as separate—I exist as a Unique Self.

I exist as an Evolutionary Unique Self that is needed, by all that is, with Outrageous Acts of Love to give that are needed in the symphony!

The whole symphony plays, and then you take out one instrument in the symphony. Then, you play the symphony again, the whole symphony is off.

---

8   *The Zohar*, Volume 10.

Then you put that instrument back in, and the entire symphony shifts. It is alive! It is beautiful again!

My friends, none of us are extras on the set. Put your voice in there, speak your voice in Unique Self Symphony, by offering up your prayer.

As we sing this prayer together, offer what you are standing for. What is your gift?

I found myself in deep communion with a presence. When I asked this presence, *What shall I call you?* (This was a presence of what I would think of as the living Christ.) The presence said, *Call me your potential self. I am you.*

In taking that to be true, the entire purpose of the life of Jesus was to incarnate the Father as a demonstration, which he said over and over and over again, *You will do the works that I did, and greater works.*

Each of us is the living presence of the living divine.

We dare to be who we truly are. I wrote the book in 1980, and I did not dare to be who I truly am until now! Well, look how long that was. I hope nobody else has to take this long to come out of the closet!

Let us give our gift to our life, ourselves, our world, and the vision of a Unique Self Symphony, in which everybody on earth, from every culture, is feeling God within, emerging as their unique expression of the Divine.

We sing to each other. We look each other in the eye, and we know, we are building something together.

CHAPTER TWO

BEAUTY AND THE BEAST: BREAKING THE SPELL OF ORDINARY LOVE

Episode 22 — March 25, 2017

PLACE ATTENTION ON THE HEART

We are here in this moment to experience the distinction between this impulse of love and creation—that is flowing through us naturally—and that which causes it to break, become destructive, cause this terrible pain in the world.

Innately, we all yearn for:

- Intimacy.
- Contact.
- Communion.
- Deep love.

So take a moment to feel that yearning for love, for creativity, for communion, for joining.

Let it rise up out of your solar plexus and go into your heart. And for a moment, just feel it expanding throughout the world.

Breathing into it together, all of us in the Evolutionary Church and way beyond.

Breathing together that love.

Now feel this scenario: Somebody comes in and criticizes you saying, *You're not good enough. You'll never make it. I don't like you!*

The local self shows up and deflates the flow of love so fast in that instant that our whole nervous system congeals in fear and anger.

The empathy is lost.

Here is the key to our continuing in our process of creation. With one flick of attention—as the energy of love gets turned off in you for whatever challenge you faced—put attention immediately back into the heart.

It's there! We first learn to breathe in the frequency of:

- Empathy
- Love
- Intimacy
- Oneness
- Wholeness

And then we discover that when a break occurs, we're in charge. **We're capable of shifting the tide internally.**

As we continue in this message of this church, we will demonstrate ways in which this larger expression of love, this Unique Self Symphony, can be cultivated individually, in small groups, and eventually worldwide.

WE ARE HOLDING THE GOOD NEWS

I just want to sing you a song, before we step into prayer, which we usually do at the end, but today it's at the beginning.

Libby Roderick, thank you very much. Turn to the person next to you and find them because we are creating our Unique Self Symphony.

We are creating not a mob, not a lynch mob. As we are going to see today, the opposite of a Unique Self Symphony is a lynch mob.

A Unique Self Symphony is Eros.
A lynch mob is pseudo-eros.

So let's just create some Eros. Let's find each other, and let's give ourselves permission to love wide and big.

We're going to sing it to each other. I invited you to sing it to the person next to you. And sing it to the person you want to sing it to. "How Could Anyone," Libby Roderick. [*See Appendix*]

Speaking to Evolutionary Church, to thousands of people around the world, we're gathering to found a new church. It's like—

> We're in Bethlehem.
> We're in Jerusalem.
> We're at the beginning.

We are not ashamed to be evangelists. But evangelist does not mean:

- That I live in some part of the Bible Belt (we love the Bible Belt, of course—let's hear it for Tennessee!)
- That I'm xenophobic or homophobic
- That you can only be saved through a particular version of speaking in tongues, by the Lord Jesus Christ, who happens not to like gay people

That is *not* what it means to be an evangelist. Evangelist means to hold the good news. It's the good news of evolution. It's the good news of evolution's personal face. It's the good news that the god you don't believe in does not exist.

INTIMACY MEANS WE ARE AWAKE AND EROTIC

God is not merely the Infinity of Power. God is the Infinity of Intimacy—and God is the intimacy that lives between Barbara and me. The intimacy that lives between Barbara and her daughter Suzanne. The intimacy that lives between David and me (Marc), the awesome David from Sunrise Ranch. The intimacy that lives between Robbie and his awesome and delightful partner.

All of that intimacy is but a reflection of the fact that we live in an intimate universe.

And if systems theory, interior sciences, complexity theory, and evolutionary science, tell us anything, it tells us that all of Reality is interconnected.

But interconnectivity, which our friend Fritjof Capra talked about—that's just the outside. **Interconnectivity is only the exterior, but the interior of interconnectivity is intimacy.** And friends, we live in an Intimate Universe. Intimacy means that we're awake and erotic.

To live an erotic life is to know that it's all intimate.

We want to live an erotic life. But to live an erotic life doesn't mean merely the sexual. We could be celibate and be living an erotic life.

The sexual models the erotic, but the erotic life is to live in Eros in every dimension of our life.

To live in intimacy in every dimension of our life, to live an erotic life, is to know that:

- It's all intimate.
- It's all interconnected.
- We impact each other, and we are held by the Divine.

Now I hate to disappoint all you New Age types—yes, we get it. *I Am God.* I didn't forget, I got it, I am God, I get it. Yes, I am the evolutionary impulse. I got it, it's all true. But friends, let's not get lost in hyper-inflated egoic narcissism. **Let's not forget that there's also a Divine beyond us.**

That knows my name.

That holds me.

That Barbara can rest in—because, my friends, if it's just *I'm God*, I lose the paradox of Rumi. Rumi, the poet, is not screaming every second, *I am God*—Rumi is saying: *I want to fall into the arms of the Beloved.*

So on the one hand, we've evolved beyond and realize, I Am—divinity lives *in* me, *as* me, and *through* me. I am the Divine, and at the same time, I'm held by God. And because I'm held by God, I can pray. **When I pray to God, I'm not giving up the grandeur and dignity of my being**—I'm saying, *I want to fall into the arms of the Beloved*—the LoveIntelligence of all of Reality that knows my name.

I'm going to tell you all a holy secret before we begin prayer. We always begin prayer with our sacred hymn. We do the same sacred hymn every week, but I want to tell you a little secret just between you and me and Barbara. A little secret, okay—for all of us who are a little lost in that New Age kind of, *it's-all-about-me*—so, ready for this?

Have you ever heard of mitosis and meiosis?

Mitosis and meiosis are these two dazzlingly complex, gorgeous symphonic processes of cellular unfolding. Mitosis and meiosis could not be thought about, could not be thought up, and could not be developed by every supercomputer in the world all combined in radical genius. And do we know that Reality manifested mitosis and meiosis before there was even a neocortex? Meaning before there's even a human being?

How did that happen? *We* didn't do it! Well, *how* did it happen?

Oh—by chance.

Really!? That's not what evolution says. **Evolution says that Reality is a story that's moving someplace. It's a story that has direction and purpose, that's intelligent and alive.**

WE ARE HELD BY THE DIVINE

So, we're going to turn in prayer. When we turn in prayer, we know that:

- The LoveIntelligence of Reality cares whether Barbara or Marc falls asleep alone or lonely at night—we might live lives of quiet desperation, but we never live lives of lonely desperation.
- We have all fallen. And every place we fall, we fall into Her (the Infinity of Intimacy's) hands.
- Every place we fall, every holy and broken *Hallelujah* of our lives, is held by the Divine.
- Nothing is lost; nothing is extra.
- In the economy of divine intimacy, everything is held, and God draws from our lips, the *holy and the broken Hallelujah*.

So as we sing the hymn of the Evolutionary Church, we offer up the Divine the details of our lives, the dignity of our personal lives, of our *holy and broken Hallelujah*. "Hallelujah," Leonard Cohen. [*See Appendix*]

When we offer our prayer, we offer up the holy and the broken *Hallelujah*.

The god we don't believe in doesn't exist. In our prayer, we affirm the dignity of personal need. In our prayer, we affirm the dignity of our *holy and our broken Hallelujah*. Sometimes *love is not a victory march. It's a cold, and it's a broken Hallelujah*. **But nothing's lost through the ecstasy, or the agony, the ecstatic urgency, or the broken moments,** and we offer up the cold and the broken *Hallelujah*, and don't miss this chance because all the gates are open.

When we pray, we affirm the dignity of personal need. I pray for Donald Trump. I pray for peace on Earth. I pray to stop demonizing Donald Trump even when we disagree with him!

TAKING THE LID OFF FOR LOVE

I (Barbara) love prayers. All these prayers are going up, and the beauty of it is: They are all being heard. I want to tell a story about what's happening here at Sunrise Ranch, in Loveland, Colorado because it is an example of what can happen. Here is the way it started. There were about a hundred members of Sunrise Ranch. They are the oldest intentional community in the United States. They have been founded by the emissaries of divine light, with a very deep—not religious, but spiritual—expression that we are creators, and as we create and give our love (with no attention to results), we change the world. And they do this, and they run the ranch.

They've invited us and others to come in to be hosts for a planetary awakening in love—a very unusual circumstance. So I will tell you how I discovered the Unique Self Symphony and how it works here.

At first, I (Barbara) was invited by the spiritual director to speak to all the members of the ranch, about a hundred people sitting on the floor in front of me. We described briefly the mission to connect co-creators worldwide, to have an Office for the Future to find out what works, and to develop a Great Library. All of those organic things.

It became my turn to speak to the members of Sunrise Ranch. And I was inspired to say, *The planetary mission—awakening in love—is your voices.*

What is required is that each of you:

- Express your unique expression, your unique gift to the planetary awakening in love.
- Take the lid off the top of your life.
- Take the lid off the top of your head when you say your unique gift to the planetary awakening.

- Don't limit it to what you could do right now, but let that heart-impulse of creativity come through you.

So the most surprising thing started to happen with the hundred people, most of whom I had not met. I was shy at first, but as I kept saying, *Take the lid off the top of your head*—because it's hard for people to recognize how much is in them, because they are not used to it—they began to take the lid off the top of their head.

People very much liked the prayers, but this was one step beyond prayer. It was, *this is my gift, and this is what I want to do*.

So it was an active agent in the process of creation. As these beautiful expressions occurred for about half an hour, David then said, *Go into small groups of three*. And in those groups, each person restates to each other, now personally with intimacy, *If I could go the whole way in my lifetime, here is what it is*.

I said: *The way I would go the whole way in my lifetime, to take the lid off is I would be able to have a global voice to invite people everywhere to give their gift into the thinking layer of Earth, which we're all on right now, into the internet, so that the collective consciousness of humanity would shift from fear to love.*

Everyone said something equally wonderful.

Then David said, *Now say it as how you would like Sunrise Ranch to express your greatness*. He made it localized, made it practical, made it what they wanted to do to make that ranch more effective and beautiful. Which they did.

After that, David said, *I think that we will never be the same again*. Because, here were a hundred people who were very efficient and going about doing their business. But we didn't know what it was like when they took the lid off the top of their heads. So recently David Kasher, the spiritual director, said, *The whole theme of the entire Sunrise Ranch could be Unique Self Symphony*.

Now, that is a hundred people coming together, doing the work of running a ranch and hosting people. The Arise Festival will be 10,000 people coming in August—all of them collectively knowing they are giving their gift to the Universe to get over the existential crisis that cannot be resolved by doing more of the same, toward an evolutionary spiritual expression of creativity and love.

So when David said, *Let's have the whole ranch recognize each human being as a member of the Unique Self Symphony*, it became necessary to ask, *Well, what should we do next?*

So, I had a little salon at my new house here, which I'm calling the Planetary Mission Central. Should you ever want to come to visit me, Planetary Mission Central is a lovely house in the midst of Sunrise Ranch, where I can have guests. So we had a small party, and I asked the people sitting in my living room what their unique gift was. It became ever more exciting, and here was the interesting insight that I want to share with you all, particularly with you, Marc.

The issue came up: how is it that there's no conductor to this symphony, and it's a self-organizing universe? **So it must be the self-organizing universe that is doing the conducting.**

It's like meiosis and mitosis—without any brains, the most complex functions like DNA or photosynthesis cannot be imagined. And it's being done through the self-organizing universe.

How does the self-organizing universe come into our own lives?

Here is what David said: *I think it's when two of the strands of that symphony feel creative with each other.* Co-creation, vocational arousal, and joining genius to create occurs because of the impulse of creativity in you, and me, and us together.

When it happens, the universe becomes self-organizing through our creativity. Because what really is creativity but the Creator within creating? So through the Unique Self Symphony, when the unique creativity turns on in you, you want that intimacy with others. It's turning on with… *you're not doing this all alone, as in an orchestra where you can't deal with anybody else.*

What we are learning—and we are going to practice this—we are going to practice having sessions of each person turning on that Unique Self Symphony, and then saying what they most need in order for that impulse to go the whole way into the universal process of creation.

What do *I* most need for my invitation to be global?

- I need media.
- I need to know to communicate.
- I need opportunity.

You know what? It's very obvious that other people in the Unique Self Symphony have exactly what's needed by me, and I have exactly what's needed by others.

The possibility of people connecting and the actual experience of creativity joining is what creates the symphony. Let's envision together—smaller groups like Sunrise Ranch, like Evolutionary Church—each expressing our unique gift to the planetary awakening in love.

The beautiful image of a Unique Self Symphony with everyone's note being heard. Join with each other to increase the creativity among the notes of a symphony to see what happens.

GET THE POWER OF UNIQUE SELF SYMPHONY

I'm going to take you all back if I can, just like six or seven years ago, when the image of the Unique Self Symphony first came to me. I (Marc) was in our Unique Self Course, the first Unique Self Course we were offering. We were trying to put this new vision of identity together in the world, and we were talking about the Unique Self as a puzzle piece.

Unique Self is a puzzle piece.
And what does a puzzle piece do?

A puzzle piece by itself, it kind of stutters around, it kind of stumbles around. But the puzzle piece *yearns* to connect to the larger puzzle. And when it connects to the larger puzzle, the puzzle pieces come together.

All of a sudden, I woke up in the middle of night. I said, Oh my God, of course. Uniqueness is not separation. **Uniqueness is the currency of connection. Uniqueness by itself makes me want to yearn.**

All of a sudden, all became clear that whether it's slime molds self-organizing, whether it's an anthill self-organizing, or at the human level:

The methodology of the self-organizing Universe is the Unique Self Symphony in which we're drawn to bring our puzzle pieces together and to create that space in between us. That's how the Unique Self Symphony works.

Because what's the strange attractor of evolution? The strange attractor of evolution is that evolution moves to more and more love, to more and more creativity, through more and more uniqueness.

When Barbara awakens to her unique puzzle piece, which is the self-organizing universe awakening, as Barbara—Reality having a Barbara experience—then Barbara is drawn through her radical uniqueness to connect.

Because the puzzle piece doesn't want to stay by itself. In the space between us, the Divine speaks.

The strange attractor of all of evolution is not just Unique Self—it is Unique Self Symphonies on the human level—which are not top-down corporations. It is not a top-down government.

It's not Trump; it's not all, *I'm the president*. It's we the people. It's the 311 number in New York, where you dial in to tell the city what needs to be repaired.

It is not The National Foundation for the Arts last year that gave $157 million dollars for the arts. It's Kickstarter—which is almost Unique Self Symphony on the web—that gave $200 million dollars.

So you begin to see the image of us coming together in the erotics of uniqueness and forming Unique Self Symphonies. But really friends, we are not there yet.

I have to tell you we are not there yet.

We do not have the Eros of it. We do not have the power of it yet. We have to model it.

At Sunrise Ranch, we're building this model of Unique Self Symphony. In the Center for Integral Wisdom, we are building this model. We are building a model in the Foundation for Conscious Evolution. We are building a model of Unique Self Symphony.

Now to really get it, you have to see what a pseudo-unique self symphony looks like. To really get the power of Unique Self Symphony, the power of its Eros, you have to see what happens when there is not real Eros. When there is not a real Unique Self Symphony—there's a pseudo-unique self symphony.

THE BEAST: A STORY OF POSTURING AND REJECTING THE ROSE

The biggest movie right now, *Beauty and the Beast*, at $170 million dollars as of a week ago, which blew out even *Batman vs Superman*, is about true superpowers. But here is the shadow scene in the movie's cartoon version, coming at you right now: Shadow Unique Self Symphony—Gaston. Here he comes, *Beauty and the Beast*.[9]

The second part of our message this week is about the biggest movie in America today. Broke all records, *Beauty and the Beast*.

What is it about, *Beauty and the Beast*? In the opening scene of the movie, there is a dance. It seems like a symphony.

There is beautiful music, but actually—

- it is all posturing,
- it is all outside,
- it is all dancing (when you are dancing your desperation, but you are not on the inside).

An old woman comes in. The old woman is not 87 years old. The old woman is 173 years old. And she walks in, and she says, *Please give me shelter for the night*.

The prince says, *No*.
He is repulsed by her.

She gives him a rose. She says, *Consider again*.
Rose is the symbol of the erotic.
Rose is the 13-petaled rose in *Kabbalah*.
Rose is Umberto Eco in *The Name of the Rose*.[10]

He says, *No*. She then reveals herself as this beautiful enchantress, and she casts a spell.

The spell is that the prince turns into a beast.

Of course, the prince is a beast:

- He cannot love the old woman

---

9 See "Beauty and the Beast—Gaston," https://youtu.be/30PVdigjbFY?si=sSI25ixi9Bgs-Nnq.
10 Umberto Eco, *The Name of the Rose*, 1980.

- He cannot receive her rose.
- He cannot give shelter to one who does not appear *to him* as his image of beauty.
- He cannot take her in, in infinite quivering tenderness.

He is a beast, and the entire dance is a sham.

The spell can only be broken under one condition. Will someone come who can love the beast? The beast will fall in love with her, and she will fall in love with him, and only if that happens will the spell be broken.

REALITY IS A LOVE STORY: THE DEEPEST STORY OF REALITY

What is the story about, my friends? *The Beauty and the Beast*. Why did it break every single record in history when it is not a movie of our times? All the reviewers said, *This is not a movie of our times; it actually goes against everything that's happening today*. Because it is the deepest story of Reality, friends, it is the deepest story.

What is the story of Reality?

What is the deepest memetic structure?

Based on all the evolutionary sciences, interior sciences, exterior—put it all together—what do we really know? Reality is a love story. The Universe is a love story.

If the Universe is a love story, and we forget how to love—or if we do ordinary love (which is a strategy of the ego) but we forget Outrageous Love (which is the Evolutionary Love that drives the whole story, that awakens in us)—then of course we're beasts.

We become beasts.

> *When we become beasts, then 17,000 children die every day of starvation, which is the truth today, when there is enough food to feed them four times over.*

When we become beasts, then 100 million people are killed in the 20th century.

Why? Because we're beasts. Because we can't love each other. Because our love is ordinary love. It's a narcissistic entitlement. It is a strategy of the ego.

BREAKING THE SPELL OF ORDINARY LOVE

When we awaken as Outrageous Love, when we awaken as the Evolutionary Eros moving in us, then the spell is broken.

When we are able to actually love and be loved, when we can see through the beast, when we can open it up, then the spell is broken.

Belle is the heroine of the movie and does not want to marry Gaston. Gaston is the preening liberal, and the preening conservative.

Gaston is the egoic one.
Gaston is playing the love game, but he's not in love.
Gaston uses love to prop up his ego.
Gaston uses love for security.

And Belle says *No* to him. When he feels rejected by Belle, because he never really loved her as she was an object of his narcissism, then he seeks to destroy her and everything precious to her, especially when he thinks that she actually has affection for the Beast.

Because true love—love is not merely an emotion—is a perception.

- To be a lover is to see with God's eyes.
- To be a lover is to see underneath.
- To be a lover is to see beneath personality.

To be a lover is to see that you are an infinitely shimmering, gorgeous, and radiant Beauty. And I see you, and I let myself be moved by you. I open myself to you, and I'm in devotion to you.

And as Belle is able to see beneath the Beast, the Beast is able to find his prince again. But Gaston feels rejected. Gaston feels like he hasn't gotten the object of his narcissism, which is Belle.

When I feel rejected, when I feel somehow like the object of my narcissism hasn't granted me my narcissistic wish, I turn into a beast.

So although the Beast seems to be in the castle, we know the Beast is not in the castle; the Beast is Gaston. And Gaston is leading the pseudo-unique self symphony. And listen.

WHAT IS A REAL UNIQUE SELF SYMPHONY?

As we all gather in erotic connection, we all gather to change the world. We all gather to change the world together, each of us committing Outrageous Acts of Love. When we don't do that, when we can't do that, the lynch mob forms. We gather in pseudo-connection, we gather in pseudo-erotic connection. And the song becomes: Kill the Beast! Kill the Beast!

Because what are we doing?

When you're in Eros, you're on the inside. When you're on the inside, there's room for everybody.

When you're not really on the inside, the only way you can have an experience of being on the inside is by placing somebody else on the outside, which gives you an illusion of being on the inside. So when Gaston can't experience real love, he says, *Kill the Beast*. He thrusts the Beast outside the circle to create the image, the pseudo-erotic mirage, and illusion of being in the circle. And that's how war starts.

War starts with the creation of an *other*, who's outside the circle.

And that's war. That's rape.

Rape is: I create an *other* without making love. I'm raping you, I'm using you, I'm abusing you.

THE PSEUDO-UNIQUE SELF SYMPHONY

Let's take the poet and turn him into a predator. Let's say that he's a danger. He's a danger to our village, he's a danger to our children!

- Let's take any new idea and murder it!
- Let's take Jesus and crucify him.
- Let's take anything that represents Eros and crucify it in order to avoid our sense of contraction and smallness.

That is the pseudo-unique self symphony, my friends.

But *imagine if instead of a war room, we had a peace room*, said my (Marc) good dear beloved whole mate Barbara Marx Hubbard 30 years ago—a peace room, a Unique Self Symphony, in which we all gather. Barbara calls it a peace room; I call it a Unique Self Symphony.

David calls it Unique Self Symphony because I don't own it, Barbara doesn't own it, and David doesn't own it. The world owns it. Let's brand it together.

Today it's all about branding, who owns it.

Nobody owns it. It's us!

The next Buddha is not one dude—the sage from the stage. It's not Barbara, it's not Marc, it's not Lisa, it's not David, and it's not Trump. The next Buddha is the *sangha*. **The next Buddha is the Unique Self Symphony.**

And it's not that we're using each other to commodify Spirit, to sell it back in a kind of New Age narcissism, surround it with pretty costumes, parade it out, and make a lot of money.

Friends, that's not the game!

What we're asking, what we're praying for, is that the Evolutionary Church be a bottom-up Unique Self Symphony. We pray that all of us together—the *sangha*—will share this with our friends.

Share it with your friends; share it with your enemies.

Make your enemies your friends.

Share it with mom and with dad, with their friends.

Let's spread this Unique Self Symphony. Let's create a bottom-up eruption and explosion of love, and let's change the world together. Can we hear that? Yeah, that's Unique Self Symphony.

We need a new song, a Unique Self Symphony song: Ben Harper's "With My Own Two Hands," as we commit our Outrageous Acts of Love. Put that record on and gave us a vision of Unique Self Symphony.[11]

Thank you, Ben! We're going to invite you to be part of church every week. I think you did a good job. Didn't he do a good job, everybody? Give him a big hand. With our own two hands, Unique Self Symphony, let's make peace on Earth.

AWAKENING IN LOVE NOW

The planetary mission has been formed to cultivate the Unique Self Symphony, such that a critical mass of voices can enter into the thinking layer of Earth, the noosphere, the media, to shift consciousness.

---

[11] Song: "With My Own Two Hands," by Ben Harper (https://www.youtube.com/watch?v=aEnfy9qfdaU).

So the beauty of our moment might never have been achieved before because there wasn't a planetary crisis of this scale, nor was there a planetary opportunity of this scale. And what we have done is put into this exact shift point, a mission for all of us, which is to connect that which is creative worldwide through a Unique Self Symphony.

So, what's hard to really catch hold of is that: This is the best way humanity can deal with the existential crisis—to connect all of us through our desire to give our gifts and to awaken our planet.

We have many different people working with us. We have media people working with us.

We have people all around the world already doing the work, wanting to work with us.

And I'd like everyone to realize that when you speak your voice into the internet, which we are all on, it is being recorded now.

We are the planet awakening.

Every one of us is awakened when we are like this. And the Unique Self Symphony is the voices of the awakening planet, being connected in the noosphere in real-time. Now.

So give your gift to the planetary shift. Every energy that is in the gift that you give is going toward the planetary awakening in love. Meaning that **all of us are shifting from fear and separation to unity and co-creation on a global scale, worldwide.** Give your gift to the planetary shift and take your part in the Unique Self Symphony.

WE NEED A STORY THAT IS EQUAL TO OUR POWER

We are calling for a planetary awakening in love through Unique Self Symphony. And we've come together with our partners at Sunrise Ranch, where I (Marc) am spending a lot of time.

We've come together with our partners in:

- Manhattan
- Carmel
- Tuscany
- Bulgaria
- Beijing
- Cambodia and Vietnam
- Japan and Taiwan
- in England. Why did you guys leave the common market, what were you guys thinking about Brexit?
- South America. We need a little Latin music in this!
- and our partners all over the world.

Right now friends, the first 5,000 people have signed up with us in the Evolutionary Church, but the Evolutionary Church has to grow. Evolutionary Church is a bottom-up Unique Self Symphony, friends. It's not Barbara, it's not Marc, it's not David, it's *all of us* together.

We can, with our own two hands, change the world. And friends, when there are five million people in the Evolutionary Church, there's a tipping point. And we will get there!

The internet by itself, friends, does nothing. It's just a technology. **And technology is dangerous as much as it offers opportunity**. Artificial intelligence offers an existential threat to our very existence. Technology is a story of power that can destroy us.

We need a story that is equal to our power.

How beautiful is that? We need a new story that's equal to our power.

That new story *is* Unique Self Symphony. That is what the new story is—a planetary awakening in love, through Unique Self Symphony.

Friends, we can actually do it together, bottom-up—not funded by a grant—funded by our love.

All people are born unique. All people are born uniquely creative. There's no one extra on the set. Reality needs our service.

Friends, let's spread the good word, let's spread the good word of Unique Self Symphony, of a planetary awakening in love.

CHAPTER THREE

REALITY INTENDED YOUR UNIQUE GIFT

Episode 23 — April 1, 2017

IMAGINE GOING THE WHOLE WAY

Welcome to the resonance of the Unique Self Symphony. This resonance has never been heard before on Earth.

It is a symphony of everyone's voice, coming from the Source of our being, vibrating with our unique greatness—our unique gift from God.

When enough of us express that uniqueness within this planetary expression, there is a harmonic that begins to self-organize. That is astonishing when we think of the harmonic of our bodies, with the 52 trillion cells, coordinated as you and me, with nobody having done that by hand. Nobody created the heart, the lungs, or the liver as a living organism. It is given fully from the Source.

Our voices—the irreducibly beautiful, unique impulse in us, as us—are placed into a Field of Intelligence, called the noosphere, such that our frequency is contributing to the awakening of the planetary nervous system in the Unique Self Symphony.

Go within and feel the vibration of that inner voice, your unique gift—the living word inside you.

- Feel it vibrate.
- Breathe into it.
- Give it life.

Take a moment to imagine it going the whole way into the noosphere. This is immediate.

We are in the noosphere. The noosphere is listening to every single person speaking our word of unique expression in resonance.

See if you can get in touch with the frequency and feeling of the voice that you would like to give to the noosphere. To begin, feel it. Then, let's say it. The noosphere is listening.

My voice, the voice within me of Conscious Evolution, is sending its vibration to awaken the noosphere collectively, to the Love-Field that is inherent in our collective voices. Send that gift into the noosphere. Let it be heard in the inner ear of evolution.

Your unique gift goes into the field of the planetary consciousness awakening in love, in resonance, in harmony. It is sent on the inner plane, heard, and given to the Book of Life for the Conscious Evolution of humanity.

STEP OUTSIDE OF OUR NARCISSISM

Outrageous Love to everyone! Oh my God!

We are living in this house together. We are *om namah Shivaya*.

We greet Lord Shiva.

We greet Christ Consciousness.

We greet Adonai Elohim.

We greet the Earth and Sky that meet.

We are greeted and held by All-That-Is.

As we move into prayer, we step out of our narcissism, and we experience ourselves as being held.

This morning, I (Marc) was delighted, honored, and privileged to be able to do a two-hour meditation. I was meditating, and when I shut my eyes, I would try to find the source of everything. I had a thought: I would go back to the beginning of my existence, I would realize, in this flash of delight, that I had done nothing to bring myself into existence.

When you have that thought, it's a shocking thought. Where did I come from? I did nothing to manifest myself.

What does that mean? **It means that I was manifested.**

Let the mind go.

Let the Eye of the Heart awaken.

Let the Eye of the Spirit open because that is what we do in prayer. We open the Eye of the Spirit and follow—it is called in *tantra*, *nimtach l'shoresho*.

We trace it back to Source. What I am tracing back to Source is myself! Where am I from? I realized that Reality intended me.

We are all the same, we are all part of the same Field of Consciousness—and we are all different, we are all held by the whole field because nothing exists independently of everything. The entire field is holding us. Literally we know—system sciences, chaos theory, complexity theory, the interior sciences—it is the truth of Reality.

Then, eyes shut, it is unbelievable, you feel the sense of *ananda*, of bliss suffuse in your entire body. I could literally feel a sense of resting and bliss. I didn't need to do it! Do you get that?

A couple of weeks ago, when I stepped onto the train, carrying my suitcase—ever had that feeling, when you are carrying a heavy suitcase, and you get on the train, and you keep carrying your heavy suitcase? Just put it down! Put it down! Rest!

I wrote a text to Barbara this morning: Let's get rid of the word *you* in Evolutionary Church. Let's just say *we*.

We, you. You, we. **We can only rest—we are a *we*—we can *only* rest, if we realize Reality intended us.** I will use the *you* word now. Reality intended you, but by *you,* I don't mean *you,* I mean *you and me.*

REALITY HEARS ME

The Reality that hears me manifested photosynthesis. All of the great minds in the world, all the great supercomputers that have won chess games against the great minds—all of them together exponentialized—could not manifest photosynthesis, this deep listening process in Reality.

Barbara didn't manifest Barbara Marx Hubbard; Reality did. Reality manifested Barbara Marx Hubbard, who is filled with a unique atomic structure, a unique cellular signature, a unique lymph node system, and an immune system unlike any other.

When Barbara talks, I hear her because the intelligence of Reality that lives in me hears Barbara, and that intelligence lives in me. This is the *pointing-out* instruction of prayer.

I shared this with my friend, Peter. He was this beautiful guy who was just blown out of his mind. He said, *Wow, I've been thinking about prayer for 30 years, now I get it.*

The intelligence that lives in me hears Barbara, but is that intelligence that lives in me limited to me? Is it just me hearing Barbara?

No, it is the intelligence that lives in me that hears Barbara.

Is that intelligence separate from the LoveIntelligence of all of Reality? Of course not.

If I can hear Barbara talk, Barbara's unique resonance, did Reality hear Barbara's unique resonance? Of course. Of course. Of course!

That is what prayer means.

Prayer means Reality hears me.

If I am responsive, if my whole system responds, does Reality respond to Barbara? Of course. If Barbara or Marc are having a lonely night (we all have lonely nights), does Reality hear that loneliness and gather me up and hold me in her arms, intending me, soothing me, and caressing me? Yes!

Is that a myth? No.

Is that fundamentalism? No.

That is the true nature of Reality: the Universe is a love story.

Ah! What do you mean, Marc? There is evil in the world.
Yes, there is evil, my friends.

I know all about evil. I am the child of a mother who was buried alive at age four, in a ghetto in Poland. I am the child of a family that was almost completely killed in World War II in one of the most horrific acts of evil. I know all about evil. I know all about betrayal.

Evil tells me that the Universe is a love story because we wouldn't even call it evil if it was not the opposite of *live*.

In other words, if Reality was not a love story, if Reality was not intimate, then evil would just be ordinary. You get it? **It's evil because it is a violation of the true nature of Reality.**

Evil is only evil because it is a failure of intimacy.

Evil itself tells me that it should not be that way. Why? Because the Universe is a love story. We are held in every moment, and our *holy and broken Hallelujah* is always held. We are never by ourselves.

Evil is just a lack of love.

Every week, we offer the song "Hallelujah", not to be entertained. We don't change this song because this song is our hymn every week. Leonard Cohen is singing the psalms of King David, in this modern rendition. Leonard Cohen—the great wild womanizer. That is who Leonard Cohen was: he was a wild, crazy womanizer, who wrote great songs, who lived a broken and a whole life, and he offered, in his songs, *the holy and the broken Hallelujah* with no pretense. To be clear, we are against womanizing because it does not honor the feminine. Leonard Cohen has to work on that, let him work on that in the next lifetime. But what we are doing is honoring Leonard Cohen. We are honoring *the holy and the broken Hallelujah* because everybody has their version of *the holy and broken Hallelujah*. "Hallelujah," Leonard Cohen [*See Appendix*]

Yeah. Amen! We are beyond. **We are beyond the place where we use each other.** We are in devotion to each other. We are in devotion to each other's fullness and to Reality, to the Divine, to the God who knows our name and holds us. Every place we fall, we fall into God's hands.

The God we don't believe in doesn't exist.

We are reclaiming prayer:

- In Evolutionary Church
- In the Evolutionary Spiritual Center
- In the Evolutionary Synagogue
- In the Evolutionary Mosque
- In the Evolutionary Buddhist Center
- In the Evolutionary Zendo
- In the Evolutionary Secular Humanist Gathering

We are reclaiming prayer for all of Reality

Can we open up our intentions? What are we for? We are for offering our prayers because prayer affirms the dignity of personal need, and we cannot bypass prayer.

I (Marc) am praying for you Barbara, to be so wildly healthy as you are now, to have the most gorgeous coming years of the most productive and stunning period of your entire life in *evolutionary partnership*. That is my prayer for you.

- We offer up prayers for livelihood.
- We offer up prayers to have all the resources necessary to give our unique gifts.
- We offer up our prayers for our sister who has cancer.
- We offer up our prayers for a person who might have had a relapse.

We don't skip prayer. We don't wait for somebody else to pray. We offer it up because all the gates are open, my friends. Yes! All the gates are open, and we offer up our prayers.

We offer up *our holy and our broken Hallelujah*, even when it all goes wrong, and for all of us, at some point, it all goes wrong. We stand before the Lord of Song, and from our lips she draws the *Hallelujah* so that we can be the people that we need to be to be in joy, to give our unique gifts that are desperately needed by All-That-Is.

Giving, not just for ourselves, we are here to evolve the source code.

We are here to create something new that has never been before. We have barely started, with thousands and thousands of people having joined from around the world. We are just starting. We are just beginning. Hold steadfast. Hold steady.

All of us together, no *you*! We, together.

IF WE DON'T THANK GOD FOR OUR GREATNESS, WHO WILL?

Yes, *amen*, indeed! Here is my question: Where are we in the evolutionary sStory? I am seeing the 13.8 billion years coming up to this moment. **In this moment of evolution, we are at the tipping point between devolution and the conscious evolution of humanity.**

We are living at the tipping point. This means that every one of us who is putting our weight toward the expression of love, of life, and the good has ten thousand times more energy in that tipping point than if we were in it fifty years ago, much less hundreds of years ago—because we are gathering, and approaching the tipping point.

What are we giving at this tipping point?

Each of us is an irreducibly beautiful expression of the entire evolutionary story of creation.

At the breaking point of evolution itself, we are summoning that immense power and letting it come through our voices. **We have been given by God the powers of godlings.** This generation has found itself at the tipping point of the tipping point, with the irreducibly beautiful, unique gift in us, with the power that we used to attribute to God, given to us as co-evolvers and co-creators of our world. This is an enormous privilege that this generation has.

The formation of the Evolutionary Church is comparable to the formation of the very early church, who believed that through their love and communion, they would experience the second coming of Christ in their lifetime. They went into the lion's den for this.

We believe that given the fact that we are on the tipping point, there is not a lot of time to stay on the tipping point. Everyone who is tipping the tipping point will—in our lifetime—experience at least the beginning of what we are calling the Unique Self Symphony.

What is a Unique Self Symphony? There would be enough voices, like every one of us, not only singing in prayer, but singing in expression of the irreducibly beautiful, infinite greatness of each of us. That is why, when we confess our greatness, we are thanking God for it.

If we don't thank God for our greatness, who will? If we don't notice our gifts, who will?

Go inside and think of the magnitude of the unique gifts we have been given—the awesome nature of them—that took 13.8 billion years to create.

We are in the first moment of conscious Unique Self Symphony. Each of our voices enters into a place where the entire system will awaken through us, as us, for us.

It may have been difficult to believe in the second coming of Christ. It may have been difficult even to believe what Teilhard said, *the Christification of the Earth*. But is it possible to believe in the planetary awakening in love?

Yes, we can do it! Definitely, we can do it! The only way we will ever do it is if we go the whole way in this lifetime. When I say the whole way, I mean that it's:

- Our prayer
- Our gift
- Our greatness
- Our love
- Our *Hallelujah*

It's our *Hallelujah* in each of us.

As my special gift in this sermon, I am going to read a few passages from the New Testament to have us consider and contemplate this extraordinarily beautiful gospel according to John.

As it says in John 1:14: *The Word Was Made Flesh*—our Word is made flesh when it is expressed as a gift to the symphony—*The Word was made flesh and dwelt among us. We beheld His glory, the glory as of the only begotten of the Father, full of grace.*

Let us place ourselves in the only begotten you, the only begotten me, full of God's grace. This is my writing about that scripture:

> Jesus perfectly represents the mind of God, the intention of Creation for this coming phase of the development of human life, as it is manifested on planet Earth, at the edge of a galaxy called the Milky Way, in a Universe of billions of galaxies.
>
> Jesus embodied the stage of being through which our consciousness must pass to enter the universal phase of co-creative life, resonating accurately with the mind of God (the Creator). Jesus embodied the next stage of a planetary civilization passing from its phase of terrestrial self-consciousness to universal co-creative consciousness.
>
> Jesus is a map of human evolution. In life, put the kingdom first and love your neighbor as yourself, forgive the sin of separation, abstain from aggressive or reactive power. In death, transcend it by gaining continuity of consciousness and a new body. In resurrection, begin your new life as a co-creator in a Universe of unlimited possibilities.
>
> The marriage of human consciousness with Christ Consciousness is natural when a species passes from creature-human to co-creator. The marriage of Christ and Eve symbolizes this union. Christ is the co-creative consciousness that already attunes directly to the will of the Creator. Christ already experiences the ecstatic love of God.
>
> —Excerpt from *The Evolutionary Testament of Co-Creation*, Barbara Marx Hubbard

That is what we were talking about in prayer: the ecstatic love of God as you. Christ experiences this. Now Eve experiences this. I don't mean only Eve in that story. It means the seeker, the one who wants to know God, which symbolizes human intellect seeking to know God through the probing of the mind in a state of self-consciousness.

I have always identified with Eve's saying, *I want to know God directly.*

> Still under the illusion that creatures are separated, Eve, the human intellect, probes to the heart of the invisible processes of Creation, the gene, the atom, the brain, the star, and is stopped by its limits. There, at the veil between the flesh and the Word, Eve calls for Christ and asks him to wed her, to transform her, joining his body to hers, transfiguring hers, carrying her beyond the limits of her five mammalian senses, to know God, and do the will of God, directly.
>
> —Excerpt from *The Evolutionary Testament of Co-Creation*, Barbara Marx Hubbard

The Unique Self Symphony—as each of us—yearns to give our voice the whole way into it and is the marriage of this separated self that seeks to know God directly with the Christ Self.

Let's charge our words with this power in the Unique Self Symphony.

GIVING YOUR UNIQUE GIFT

What does it mean to give your unique gift in the Unique Self Symphony?

The Unique Self Symphony is the new image of Reality.

They used to fix New York, when New York was all broken down. There was an office in New York where they sent people to figure out what was wrong. They created a phone number 311. In New York, you dial 311 and say, *Hey, this needs fixing in the city!* All of a sudden the entire city is participating together in healing and transforming New York. It is not top-down anymore.

There is the beginning of an enacted symphony. I am speaking to what needs *Tikkun. Tikkun* means:

- What needs fixing?
- What needs healing?
- What needs transformation?

It used to be, if you wanted to have an art project, you would go to the National Endowment for the Arts and put in an application. Last year, or the year before, they raised a couple hundred million dollars, because with Kickstarter they can raise $250 million when people get on the internet and create a Unique Self Symphony. They are offering art into the world. It is a new world!

NO ONE EVOLVES BEYOND EGO

Let's clarify Unique Self. Our Unique Self Symphonies aren't clarified because we don't really yet know what a Unique Self is. To get to my Unique Self, I have to liberate my ego. I have to evolve beyond exclusive identification with ego.

You never evolve beyond ego. If you evolve beyond ego, you are pathological.

Never evolve beyond ego, holy friends. You evolve beyond exclusive identification with ego.

Ego becomes a voice, not a veto. We say, *oh, that is the ego's voice, that is a healthy voice*. It drives us forward, but we are not identified with ego. Do you get that distinction? It is a great distinction. Evolve beyond exclusive identification with ego. I have known, in my history, that whenever I see teachers and systems saying, *evolve beyond ego*, it means all the ego, all the shadow is hidden. You can't have a conversation because no one has ego, no one has shadow. When people say, *We have evolved beyond ego*, beware!

No one evolves beyond ego.

- Ramana Maharshi had an ego.
- Jesus had an ego.
- Buddha had an ego.
- Barbara Marx Hubbard has an ego.
- Marc has an ego.
- Ken Wilber has an ego.

There is no one who doesn't have an ego. It's just that we don't identify with ego. When we evolve beyond exclusive identification with the ego, then we can find Unique Self.

A STORY ABOUT UNIQUE GIFT: SLIPPING YOUR ENVELOPE UNDER THE DOOR

I am going to tell you a story. Instead of talking about the *dharma*, I want to tell you a story. Are you ready for a story?

It is a unique gift story:

> I was in Kraków a few years ago, and I was there with a shamanic friend. We were there to clear the land—to the extent possible shamanically—of the impact, of the tragedies, of the massacres in Europe. It was an esoteric, shamanic trip.
>
> I was in study, learning the art of clearing land and freeing souls. We were going to different cemeteries in Europe, trying to liberate the souls that were stuck in different cemeteries. At that point in my life, I was thinking about what I would like to spend the rest of my life doing. Would I be totally anonymous, wander the world quietly, clear land and free souls and cemeteries?

I had a beautiful teacher, and we talked about me taking over that lineage, being a successor. The reason I did not do it: I was not that good at it.

I could never figure out whether the soul was actually freed or not, had we cleared the land or not. I would think I had completely cleared it, and my teacher would say, *No, I did not do it*. I could never figure out what was actually going on. I figured, I am not such a good soul-freer. Let me try something else. What can I do? I still try to live in that realm, in the subtle realm.

We are in Kraków, and in Kraków, there is a great mystical story. There is a grave. We went to the Jewish cemetery in Kraków, which is near Auschwitz. We were on our way to Auschwitz, the concentration camp, and there is a cemetery. There is a man buried in the cemetery, and on his tombstone it says, *Sham nitman Yossele kamtzan kodesh*—Here is buried Yossele, the Holy Miser.

This is how you identify your unique gift.

That's what the story's about. Who is Yossele, the Holy Miser, buried in the Kraków cemetery? You never know who a person is, you never know, you never know, you never know. Who might be one of the thirty-six men and women, upon whom the world stands?

You never know, is it Barbara Marx Hubbard?

Is it an anonymous person who is changing the sheets in your hotel room?

It could be one of the poles. In Sufism, there are people who are poles that connect Heaven and Earth.

It could be a street cleaner.

It could be a holy miser.

Yossele, the Holy Miser, was in a Kraków ghetto in the 16th century. He was one of the wealthiest men, but he wouldn't give any money away. (In a Hebrew community, in the 16th century, not giving money to support other people in the ghetto was a disaster. It was not about philanthropy; your money was not your money. Your money was part of the community; it was not yours.)

Yossele, who refused to help everyone, was on his deathbed. He was 117 years old. He was on his deathbed. People came to him and said, *Listen, you have to give some money to the community because if you don't, we are not going to bury you.*

And he said, *I lived my life alone. I'll bury myself. Get out of here!*

He threw everyone out, and he died the next day. The people from the burial society—the *chevre kadisha*, or the holy gathering—refused to bury him because he hadn't been a good human being his whole life. He refused to help everyone, so they left him in his house. One day, two days, three days, finally on the third day, someone snuck into his house and put his body over their shoulder and brought him to the edge of the cemetery and buried him.

Then my friends, open your hearts, listen to this:

It is Friday morning. What happens on Friday morning? There is a little knock at the door of the house of the Rabbi.

Man: *Oh, could I have a little loan?*

Rabbi: *Why do you need a loan?*

Man: *So I'll have money for the Sabbath meal for my family.*

Rabbi: *Of course, I'll give you a loan. But what have you been doing till now?*

Man: *Well, I always used to get a little envelope under my door. And in that envelope every week there was like ten kopecks, and this week the envelope didn't come.*

Seemed strange to the Rabbi, but he says, *okay*, and the man goes away.

Knock, knock. Someone else knocks at the door.

Rabbi: *What do you need?*

Man #2: *Oh, I need 15 kopecks in order to have food for my family for the Sabbath.*

Rabbi: *Well, of course, I'll give you 15 kopecks. But where were you last week?*

Man #2: *Well, every week, I would get an envelope under my door, but this week there was no envelope.*

Rabbi: *That's very strange. How did that happen? What a strange coincidence, two people!*

He gives him 15 kopecks with delight and sends him on his way.

And then another knock.

Man #3: *Could I have seven kopecks?*

Rabbi: *Where were you last week?*

Man #3: *Well, last week, I found an envelope under my door.*

Knocks at the door continued until there were thirty-seven people, more and more. All the poor people of the ghetto in Kraków come to ask the rabbi for a little money for buying food and wine for the Sabbath meals.

What did they realize? They realized they had all received envelopes under their door, and then one of them remembered a story. They all remembered a similar story. It is a story within a story.

One of them remembers twenty-five years prior and shares the story:

When I first became poor, I said to myself, *I am desperate, maybe I'll go to the home of Yossele, the Miser. We know he doesn't give money, but maybe he'll give me some money.* So I knocked at the door, Yossele gave me a big smile, and he welcomed me. He gave me sponge cake and a shot of vodka. He said, *Who are you, and where do you live? How many children do you have? How much money do you need a week?*

I thought he was open to me, so I said, *Thank you for asking all these questions. Could you please give me a few kopecks?* Then, Yossele looked at me, and his face went white, then red. He was livid with rage, or so it seemed. He picked me up. He was a big, huge man. He threw me down the steps. I was so traumatized. I was so ashamed. I didn't even tell my wife what happened. I went on my way and never told anyone. I forgot about it.

Now that I think about it, a few weeks later, maybe two months later, I started getting notes and an envelope under my door. I started getting envelopes that had the right amount of money that I needed. Now, I realized it was Yossele.

All the people in the town start crying out: *Oh Yossele! Yossele! Yossele, forgive us! Forgive us! We didn't know who you were! Yossele, forgive us! We didn't recognize you! Yossele, we didn't know!*

The Rabbi gathers all the people in the town. They all come into the square, and they pray for forgiveness, for not having seen who Yossele was. The Rabbi is in the middle of this prayer, and he falls down, Ah! He falls down into a faint. He goes up to the highest heaven, and he sees Yossele there smiling.

Rabbi: *Forgive us, forgive us!*

Yossele: *No forgiveness is necessary.*

Rabbi: *We didn't bury you! We weren't at your funeral.*

Yossele: *It doesn't matter. At my funeral were every great master. Jesus was at my funeral—I didn't know that Jesus could be at a Jewish funeral—and Moses was at my funeral, and Buddha was at my funeral, and all the great masters. They were all at my funeral, and they all buried me together. It was the most beautiful place, and I'm now sitting by the Divine Throne in bliss and eternity.*

Rabbi: *Oh my god we didn't know you, we didn't know you! But Yossele, you don't look so happy.*

Yossele: *Well, I'm in bliss, I'm in eternity. But I have to say, Rabbi, if only I could be back on Earth for one Friday morning to put envelopes under people's doors, one more week.*

YOU IDENTIFY YOUR UNIQUE GIFT

My friends, we all have envelopes to put under people's doors. You know how you identify your unique gift? It is the envelope that you have to slip under someone's door.

- It might be public.
- It might be anonymous.
- It might be starting a planetary mission.
- It might be helping in a particular unique and gorgeous way, someone in your circle of intimacy and influence, in a way that no one else can help them.

We all have envelopes, and our envelopes are not about being public. They are not about drama. They are not even about being a leading innovator, doing something worldwide. You might be a leading innovator, but you might be, like most of us, a Unique Self, living your life with your *holy and your broken Hallelujah.*

And the Unique Self Symphony, or what we call Wheel 2.0, are innovators worldwide, who come together.

Every single Unique Self gives their gift and affects the entire Wheel of Co-Creation by slipping under the door that envelope that is theirs to give.

Friends, there is no bliss, there is no eternity, that is as beautiful as knowing you can put ten kopecks in an envelope and slip it under a friend's door and have your heart blown open.

I have a gift to give. I can change the world!

Evolution is love in action.

CHAPTER FOUR

ATTUNING AND RESPONDING TO OUTRAGEOUS LOVE IN A SELF-ORGANIZING UNIVERSE

Episode 24 — April 8, 2017

This is an outrageous day! An outrageous day is when we are willing to incarnate Outrageous Love as the Eros of evolution awakening in us and as us.

I am going to evoke the full-scale embodiment of the Eros of evolution as us. It comes from an unpublished book called *Laws of Outrageous Love: The Essence of the Unique Self Symphony.*

Imagine the love inside you as a pulsing expression of the genius of the 13.8 billion years of evolution, incarnating uniquely as you.

Feel into the feeling of your love, not your ordinary love of one another, but the passion that motivates you to:

- Be more
- Love more
- Create more
- Express more of the Divine essence of *you*.

Feel the evolutionary impulse of evolution as Eros. Breathe up into that unique expression of divine love. **Imagine the glory that could be heard, that will be heard, that is being heard, as a critical mass of humanity expresses their Outrageous Love as their note in the Unique Self Symphony, within the nervous system of humanity.**

We allow ourselves in this resonance to feel each other's presence.

Everyone has an expression of evolution activating it, breathing into it. We are the Unique Self Symphony. We are not waiting for some special event; we *are* the special event now!

OUTRAGEOUS LOVE DRIVES EVERYTHING

We are in this great convocation together. We are in Bethlehem. We are the co-founders of the new church. We are in biblical times, literally. You can feel the quickening all around us. You can feel the pulsating all around us.

There are times when hundreds, thousands, millions, and even billions of years go by with almost imperceptible changes, and evolutionary time is moving slowly, so slowly you barely perceive that it is moving at all. And then, there are biblical times.

Biblical times are times of quickening.

This is a time of quickening pulses. Ray Kurzweil, our colleague, talks about the exponential increase in change.

Imagine the world of our great-grandparents. It was fundamentally different from our world, and also in a way that was not true about the world of *their* great-grandparents.

Do you understand?

In other words, for a thousand years, very little moved in Europe. It was basically the same world for two thousand, even three thousand years.

Now, all of a sudden we live in a world so different from our great-great-grandparents. They had no cars, telephones, or faxes. **We live in an interconnected world of jet travel, nanotechnology, and emergent technologies with powers beyond imagination at our fingertips.**

We live in a world in which the average human being with a cell phone has available to them more connectivity and information than the most powerful man in the world did 100 years ago.

Our cell phones are becoming part of us. We are living in this emergent world of rapid change. In this emergent world of rapid change, there is something that is both holding it all and driving it all.

We need a unique response to it all in order to evolve it, and make it work, and invest this world with the qualities that will bring it to usher in a heaven on Earth, instead of a disaster beyond imagination in human history.

What is that quality?
How do we create a new politics of Outrageous Love?
How do we create a new politics of transformation?

The answer is—as we have been saying, let's create an Evolutionary Church, which is a synagogue, a mosque, and a spiritual center where:

- That which unites us is much greater than that which divides us
- There are new tenets, new creeds of faith
- We are faithful to the future
- We have a vision of what Reality is

We want to convene our Unique Self Symphony, which is a self-organizing Universe, based on Unique Selves each giving their gifts into Reality, linking together in shared projects and shared visions of a bottom-up self-organizing Universe—a Unique Self Symphony.

What drives the Unique Self Symphony? What makes it go? What kind of love do we need to make Unique Self Symphony actually play its music?

Reality is Outrageous Love. **Outrageous Love drives everything all the way up and all the way down the evolutionary chain.**

We need not ordinary love but Outrageous Love. Ordinary love is the love which is a strategy of the ego. Ordinary love masquerades as love, but it is not really love. It is incoherent when you look at the wave pattern of ordinary love.

Outrageous Love is the way we love other human beings, for sure, but Outrageous Love is also the way that molecules love each other.

It is when we don't love each other as a strategy of the ego but instead feel Outrageous Love: the love that drives all of Reality, that is all of Reality. Outrageous Love is the intimacy that holds everything together.

Outrageous Love is the force of attraction and allurement that holds it all together, on the one hand, and it is the force that drives it all forward, on the other hand.

It is the *Becoming*. It's the ecstatic urgency of Cosmos, the evolutionary Eros embodied in us, as us, and through us. It is that which attracts us and allures us and holds us together.

YOUR PERSONAL QUALITY PARTICIPATES IN GOD'S PERSONAL QUALITY

We set the resonant Field of Outrageous Love, in this historic moment, as they were in Bethlehem. We are at this biblical time of quickening, where we are convening together.

- It is us.
- It is our turn.
- We are the new Renaissance.

- It is going to emerge out and ripple out.
- We are the ones.
- It is our turn.

As we articulate and incarnate the politics of Evolutionary and Outrageous Love, we ask ourselves questions:

How do we step into prayer?

Who is God in this story?

Remember, the god you don't believe in does not exist. It's not *God is love* exactly—God is Outrageous Love! What we mean by that force of Outrageous Love we described is Divinity. That is what we mean by Divinity.

Outrageous Love is not an impersonal force. It is not merely the ceaseless creativity of Cosmos. It is not an impersonal evolutionary impulse. **Outrageous Love is an evolutionary impulse that is suffused with personhood.**

As you feel a friend talk, do you feel their uniqueness? I do, and it moves me every time.

That personal quality is the personal intimate quality of Outrageous Love. And, that personal quality participates in Divinity, participates in God, because God is the infinitely personal intimate quality of Cosmos, which is the inside, the interior, of Outrageous Love. **Outrageous Love surges forward, and it is infinitely intimate**.

That's why Outrageous Love is not just this surging Infinity of Power. It is the Infinity of Intimacy that knows our name and holds us, in every broken moment and every whole moment, in every broken *Hallelujah* and every holy *Hallelujah*.

There is no moment of our lives in which we are left separate. There is no moment of our lives in which we are apart. There is no moment of our lives in which we are alone.

- Prayer affirms the dignity of our lives.
- Prayer affirms the dignity of our personal need.
- Pray for our brokenness and our wholeness together, and that Outrageous Love knows our name and holds us in every moment.

It is not that we go beyond our loneliness. We never bypass our loneliness. We dissolve our loneliness, knowing that we are being held and madly adored, ecstatically loved—personally—by all of Reality in every moment.

We are excited! Are we evangelicals? We are evangelicals.

What kind of evangelicals? Evolutionary evangelicals!

And what is the good news?

It is the good news, not of ordinary love, not the strategy of the ego that we call love. It is the good news of Outrageous Love—the God that holds us and lives as us. We are together, Outrageous Lovers, articulating and praying our *holy and broken Hallelujahs*.

That song is what we pray with.

It doesn't matter if we messed up little things along the way.

It doesn't matter if we messed up some big things along the way because we are all making mistakes, my friends, and we are all that little child. See if you can find that little child in yourself. Let's find that little child in ourselves.

Whenever we make a little mistake, we remonstrate ourselves. We are all looking in the wrong direction sometimes, but we are all offering *our holy and our broken Hallelujah*. **We all make mistakes, but we are making mistakes in the right direction**. The Hebrew word for return, repent, transform is *teshuva*. What it means is, you turn your face to the right direction. Make mistakes in the right direction.

The gates of prayer are never closed. You are the prayer—be prayer! Let's be holy shakers and holy bringers of the good news. Let's laugh at ourselves the whole way. In other words, we take ourselves radically seriously, and we laugh at the same time.

Find your way in a way you never have. You are the prayer—be prayer!

It's the promise of all the great traditions: on the Inside of the Inside, when you go and write or speak your prayer, or speak at home to yourself, the gates open—**even if all the gates are closed, the gates of prayer are never closed.**

How do we awaken, embody this, and make this real? The gates of prayer are open. We are here. The tears are flowing; our hearts are open. Oh my God!

EMBODIED AWARENESS OF OUTRAGEOUS LOVE: FEELING THE WHOLE STORY OF CREATION

Here is a gorgeous paragraph from our unpublished book, *Laws of Outrageous Love*.

Here it is, and this is what we are going to embody. I am going to read it, even as I am embodying and reading it.

> *Outrageous Love is the pulsating, erotic LoveIntelligence that initiated the great flaring forth of Reality. It is the force of allurement and attraction that moves all of existence.*

Our friend, Andrew Cohen, said, *the Big Bang is still banging within us*. It is not one Big Bang. It is a continuous process inside of us.

You know our phrase, *The Universe: A Love Story*? What does that mean? It means from the very moment of creation, particles attracted to particles, quarks to quarks, electrons to electrons, protons to protons, all the way up to us.

All the way on up to you and me.

We embody the force of allurement and attraction that moves all of existence.

We would like everyone to embody this.

EVOLUTIONARY CHAKRA MEDITATION

The *Evolutionary Chakra Meditation* is the pulsing, erotic expression of divine intent, starting 13.8 billion years ago.

We go through those first 13.8 billion years until we get to us.

Breathe into that.

> *Breathe into the origin of creation, and go before that into consciousness itself, out of which the Big Bang of supreme intelligence arose.*

The Field of Consciousness initiated an origin of life, coded in those first three seconds, with the exquisite design of energy, matter, and life. If that Big Bang had not been, we would not be here.

THE UNIVERSE IS PERFECTLY ATTUNED FOR LIFE

When we use the word attunement, let's go to its origin in the Big Bang. Let's go even deeper than that! Let's go to the consciousness out of which the Big Bang has emerged and created the Universe.

As Brian Swimme once said, *The Universe always wants more*. It could have been satisfied with hydrogen, but no, why did it want galaxies? Why did it want all the universal process of creation turning into the rock of Earth?

Folks, the rock of Earth was a huge achievement, they say about 3.7 billion years ago. What happened on the rock of Earth with this impulse of creation? Life, amazing, creative life emerged. The DNA coded and exchanged codes all throughout this rock. That code of DNA in us has that experience!

If life could do that, what can it do now? This is the origin of the expectancy. **This is the origin of radical expectancy that comes from universal creativity.** So, I will skip quickly through the rock of Earth, the origin of life, the origin of single-celled life, and the origin of multicellular life.

Let's go to the bringing in of solar energy into life on Earth with single-celled life. Solar energy for billions of years was a poison. What happened to handle the poison of solar energy? Multicellular life! Multicellular life and solar energy has helped to populate the world. This has a lot to tell us.

What is going to handle the poison that is coming through us? It is a multi-connected love of each other!

I would like to get to this amazing story of the origin of humans. What is this impulse going through those early humans? They had no idea of *Homo erectus, Homo habilis, Homo neanderthal*. And then *Homo sapiens sapiens*—us—we have to put ourselves in the lineage that we belong in. Do not worry about which creed or color you are; this is who you are—take the whole origin as yours! Everybody is a human body-mind-spirit created by this entire process of creation.

We look at the origin of creation and take the entire impulse of the consciousness force as a glowing spiral of evolutionary light and bring it into your lower chakra—your security chakra. Let the entire 13.8 billion years of coding come into your lowest chakra and feel it there as your security.

If you ever doubt that you have this capacity for security within yourself, just remember you are incarnating the 13.8 billion years of intelligence. Breathe up through the entire mind of God, up to 13.8 billion years.

Now, get to the generative organs, which creates new life in the feminine and the masculine. Invite the impulse of evolution to move from massive procreation to co-creation inside you, awakening your creativity. Imagine that you are shifting from degeneration toward regeneration by including, inside yourself, this impulse of evolution.

For years, this has been what moves me toward regeneration.

Why? Because I have more to do.

If you feel you have more to do with your impulse of evolution, ask it to evolve you into a form of regeneration in which the very cellular life begins to feel it has more to do and turns on. Then you get newer every day rather than older. Yes, the body ages, but you do not.

Take the impulse, breathe it from the mind of God, all the way on up through, and bring it into your solar plexus, into your power center.

Would you like to ask the impulse of evolution to empower you to fulfill your divine intelligence and give it out from your power center into the world? If so, ask and it is given, knock and doors are opening now.

We are doing this for the very first time. **We are hosting billions of years of evolution inside our own body-minds.** This has now exploded into the process of creation through us.

Now, take it up! I have created this little extra chakra called your lower heart. Does anybody have conflicted emotions? Does anybody ever feel distressed? *I don't like this. I don't like that. I'm not happy here.*

You know what? I invite you to invite the impulse of evolution right up through those distressed emotions and have the impulse of evolution orient them in a direction.

> *Is the impulse of evolution directional? It went from subatomic particles to us. Of course it is directional. Of course it is intentional.*

Of course, it has purpose, or it couldn't be sitting here in us. It couldn't be done accidentally, impossible!

Ask that impulse to orient every single emotion that feels slightly off-center and take it, orient it, put it into your lower heart. In your lower heart, feel Outrageous Love in the sense of the infinite erotic pulsing love that creates our entire Universe!

The upper heart is your vocation. It is your vocation in the original sense of the word, *Vocare*. It is your gift to give to the world. Take the impulse of evolution up into the upper heart.

Bring up your gift to give it to the world. From that upper heart, give it out as your vocation. Your unique, brilliant beauty is outrageously powerful. Don't forget that!

Breathe that from the mind of God, all the way.

Take it up into your throat. In your throat is the vibrational Field of Evolution coming through you. Do not just say, *Hi there, how are you?* No! You are breathing in from the mind of God, all the way on up.

I am the voice of Conscious Evolution speaking.

When you speak with each other in your unique vocation, be the voice of the consciously evolving you!

Take that beautiful voice and bring it up into the third eye. Have passionate intuition as the emerging culture that we are co-creating in the evolving humanity. In the synagogues, temples, mosques, cathedrals, centers, everywhere, we are evolving to the highest level!

Then bring it up, out to the top of your head. I bring here what I call the "Universal Human." I bring us to post-transition. We made it through folks. We are on the other side of the planetary shift. We are universal humans:

- We are alive.
- We are well.
- We are here.

We take one more deep breath and breathe it all the way back down. Breathe it down into the mind of God and breathe it up, once again, into the field.

RESPONDING TO A POLITICS OF DEVOLUTION WITH A POLITICS OF EVOLUTION

How do we embody the Evolutionary Eros? Another name for Outrageous Love is the Evolutionary Eros that moves all the way up and all the way down. In the evolutionary meditation, we went up through the centers of cultural consciousness. It goes from the beginning of the subatomic:

- All the way up to the cellular level
- All the way up to the cultural level
- All the way up to all the personal levels that live in us

Where are we? Are we in a casual, New Age, human-potential activity, which is filling up a little time on a Saturday morning? I do not think so!

Where are we? We are convening together to bring the good word! Our response to a politics of devolution is a politics of evolution.

Our response:

- To fragmentation
- To pettiness,
- To contraction,
- To a failure of leadership...

...is to become the leaders ourselves, to become Unique Self expressions of the self-organizing universe, in order to enact a Unique Self Symphony, which is a self-organizing universe.

Self-organization means intelligence. Self-organization means it is going somewhere. Self-organization means there is a story that has direction. Self-organization means we want to get there. We want to come home. We want to create heaven on Earth.

How do we create Heaven on Earth?

Not through a top-down corporate structure, but through a bottom-up structure in which everyone is giving their gift and speaking their voice into the Unique Self Symphony as Unique Self.

How does a Unique Self Symphony happen? It happens in one way and one way only: through Outrageous Love.

You have to feel Outrageous Love moving inside you. You have to be drunk. If not, you cannot play your Unique Self instrument—we cannot play our Unique Self instrument. This is the essence of the whole thing, without this, nothing moves, nothing happens. It's just words. It's just all words.

Here is the core, the core of everything: you have to feel Outrageous Love moving inside you. You have to be drunk.

I remember spending a night with Coleman Barks at a huge event. Coleman Barks is the man who brought together the Rumi poems and re-illuminated them. Rumi is drunk with Divinity.

You have to be drunk with the evolutionary impulse. You cannot do this sober. I want to make that really clear.

Stay in your 12-step, and I'll stay in my 12-step program. I don't have one, but we all should because we all have some form of addiction. And let's liberate our addictions. Fantastic!

Let's get drunk! We have to get drunk with the evolutionary impulse. We have to get drunk with ecstatic urgency. We have to be intoxicated. It will not happen if:

- If we're not intoxicated with evolution
- If we're not God-intoxicated
- If we don't feel the vineyard flowing through us

And that is the word: Outrageous Love. It is why we use the word *Outrageous* because it's outrageous! This is not this sweet little activity we do. But, this is about saying:

- Oh my god, I am drunk!
- I have a passion to give my unique gift.
- I am urgently driven.
- It is an erotic drive in me.

I do not want my life to wind up being a *tale told by an idiot, full of sound and fury, signifying nothing*. I want to live a life that matters. I want to play a larger game.

We are all Superman, and although we all have our kryptonite, we all have superpowers!

We have *our holy and our broken Hallelujah*. We have the unique gift that all of Reality waits for us to give. We have the unique poem that is ours to write. We have a unique life that is ours to live.

By living that unique life, we are intoxicated with Outrageous Love! **We are giving those gifts, making something happen, and addressing a unique need in our unique circle of intimacy and influence.** That is how Outrageous Love flows.

Outrageous Love is outrageous. It is not ordinary. It is not average. It is not conventional. It's outrageous!

If you can, find that part of you that starts dancing in the shower, picks up an imaginary microphone, and starts doing this massive concert for a billion people. That part of you that sings in the shower, that part of you who is silly and wild and delightful, that part of you is outrageous!

Remember that child who dreamed? You remember how far you wanted to reach? It is not about how it plays in the particular public sphere. **It's about finding, in yourself, that child who is outrageous.**

Outrageous, in the most beautiful way, not outrageous in a negative way. Outrageous, which is the full explosion. The drunken explosion of your sobriety.

If we get really sober—people say, let's take a sober look at the issues surrounding us in the world.

We say: No, no let's take a drunken look at the issues surrounding us in the world!

Do you get what I mean? Of course we want to be sober. We have to be drunk in our sobriety, in our seriousness. We have to be filled.

When you are ecstatic, you can change everything.

When you are contracted, scared, alone, and lonely—we all know those emotions—know that the Outrageous Love is with you!

In knowing that, and in feeling that intimacy knowing our name, and picking us up and holding us, we find the *outrageous* again.

We must weave together a new *dharma*:

- The new vision
- The new story

- The new evolutionary story
- The new sacred texts

We must write a new library of sacred texts, stories, and prayers from Unique Self and Outrageous Love.

When we tell a story, it is not casual; it is a sacred story. I am going to go back several times over the next year to the stories that we have told and then interpret them, so they become part of our sacred canon.

TO LIFE! THE STORY OF YANKELE

We need new stories. We need new stories about the Apostles, new stories about the initiates because:

- We are the Apostles.
- We are the initiates.
- We are the Buddhas.
- We are the Arhats.
- We are the Bodhisattvas.

It's us!

And, new stories!

We can let the scariness go because we feel the Outrageous Love living in us.

Here is the core story—this is the *feeling* of Outrageous Love:

It is a story about this man who comes to his master, and it's the eve of *Yom Kippur*. Those of you who don't know any Jews, that is called the *Day of Atonement*.

If you are Jewish, you might know that. If you are Buddhist, it works. If you are Christian, it works.

We take from all the holy days and from all the traditions. In evolutionary science, we say that there is not one center, there are multiple centers.

- Judaism is the center of everything.
- Christianity is the center of everything.
- Islam is the center of everything.
- Buddhism is the center of everything.
- Secular Humanism is the center of everything.

In evolutionary science, there are multiple centers. Here is the story:

A man named Yankele comes to his master. It is the Day of Atonement, and his master said to him: *Get out of here. Get out of here.*

The man says: *What do you mean, why should I get out of here?*

Master says: *Because you are going to die, and if you die on this holiday, you are going to ruin my holiday.* (And that's not a very good thing for a master to say. Clearly, he did not go to pastor school.)

The man is kind of brokenhearted. He's been the disciple of this master forever. He leaves town, and he is kind of broken, walking along, and he sees his friends coming by in a wagon, a horse-drawn wagon, as they would drive in those days in the mid-19th century, on the trails of the settlement in Russia.

His friends were also going to the master for this holy day, and they said, *you don't look good, Yankele, you look a little depressed and sad.*

He said, *I know, I went to the master and he threw me, he threw me out, and he said I'm going to die today!*

So, his friends said, *Well if that's the case, we are before the holiday, and you don't really need your money, so why don't you invite us for a drink?* Because after all, you are going to die, and you know, you should treat us well.

That doesn't seem so polite either, but that's what his friends said. He had nothing else to do, so they went into a local tavern.

His friends say to him, *Buy us a drink.* So he buys everyone a round. What does he have to do with his money anyway? They all raised their glasses, and they drink:

L'chaim—*l'chaim* means to life—*salud* to life. They all drink it up! *Let's drink up!*

That was good whiskey going down.

Well, what do you mean by one round?

You don't need your money. Buy us, the friends say, *another round.* So, they pour everybody another round. Everyone raises their glasses, *l'chaim*, to life.

Everyone drink it up, drink it up, everyone! They drink it up, and then they do a third round. *Everyone drink up, hold up your glasses, drink it up*: *l'chaim*, to life.

And a fourth round: *l'chaim*, to life. And a fifth round: *l'chaim*, to life. They are drinking; now they're up to the tenth round. And they're up to the eleventh round, and they are drunk, and they are gone!

They are stumbling out of the tavern.)Thank God they didn't have to drink and drive cars. You can't drive a wagon that poorly when you're drunk.)

They get to the Master's place, and they look at the time. Oh my god! It is time for the Day of Atonement. It is about to begin, and they go into the master's inner study; they just stumble their way in, drunk.

The master looks at Yankele, who he said several hours ago was going to die. He says, *Yankele, the angel of death has left. You are going to live. You are going to live and have the most beautiful year of your life coming up!*

Yankele said, *I don't understand. You are the master. You are the great seer. You can see from one end of the world to the other. You told me I was going to die, and you are never wrong.*

Open your hearts—the master said to him. *Don't you understand? I'm the master; I'm just one.*

But when the whole community comes together, and the community cries out together *l'chaim*, to life, that crying out of the community—which is the Unique Self Symphony—comes together in drunken intoxication, screaming out together, to life, then **all decrees of death are averted; all decrees of destruction are averted.**

We stand not before the potential personal death of any human being. We stand before the possible extinction of life as we know it.

TO FACE EXISTENTIAL THREAT, YOU HAVE TO FEEL OUTRAGEOUS LOVE

The existential threat is real, not in a doomsday sense, in a simple reality sense. The seven or eight vectors, which pose grave existential risk to the very future of life on this planet, are absolutely real.

The only response to that outrageous pain is Outrageous Love.

> *We live in a world of outrageous pain, and the only response is Outrageous Love.*

You have to feel. You have to embody. We have to embody—all of us—the Evolutionary Eros and the Outrageous Love moving up through us.

Then we have to feel the impulse alive, demanding, drunk inside of us. We cry out with Outrageous Love.

It is outrageous!

It breaks every boundary but not appropriate boundaries. We keep every appropriate boundary. When you break a boundary, you are breaking the boundary of your contraction.

We are breaking the boundary of our smallness.

We are breaking the boundary that prevents us from crying out to all of Reality with the deepest force within us: *l'chaim*. To life. To life. To life. To life!

We raise our glasses together as Outrageous Lovers having experienced a gorgeous Evolutionary Chakra Meditation. And we say:

- We are Outrageous Lovers.
- We are the Unique Self Symphony.
- It is not ordinary love that powers Unique Self Symphony; it is Outrageous Love.

Outrageous Love isn't just an emotion. **Outrageous Love is a perception, which means you can see with God's eyes**. You have evolutionary eyes. You can see—Reality needs us.

CHAPTER FIVE

OUR SIX CORE ESSENTIAL HUMAN NEEDS

Episode 25 — April 15, 2017

THE WEDDING DAY OF THE ESSENTIAL SELF WITH THE UNIVERSAL SELF

Easter, resurrection day. One of the codes in *52 Codes for Conscious Self Evolution*[12] is: You are entering an extended wedding day of the Essential Self and the Universal Self.

Let's tune in to the Essential Self—the soul's code—the Unique Self that is an expression of the whole process of creation awakening. **The Essential Self is alive and needs to contact its own higher self, its Universal Self, the highest frequency of its being.**

Let's place attention on essence—the soul's code—the evolutionary impulse in you. Breathing deeply into the impulse. Feel it coming from the source of creation. Let that impulse come from the mind of God through the billions and billions of years. Experience it emerging as your essence.

---

12 Barbara Marx Hubbard, *52 Codes for Conscious Self Evolution: A Process of Metamorphosis* (Ashland, OR: Foundation for Conscious Evolution, 2010).

What does your essence really need, in order to belong fully? Your essence needs union with its own universal highest frequency—its Divine Self—its Christ Self.

Place your attention on:

- Essence
- The soul's yearning for full manifestation and expression
- The impulse of evolution coming through you in all its power

Allow it to attract into itself the highest frequency of your being:

- Universal Self
- Post-transition Self
- Already emergent Self
- Fully potentiated Self

Draw on the field of the living Christ.

Bring it in to join Essential Self in this resonance until the very frequencies of your body, mind, heart, and spirit are lifted up by that highest frequency in your Universal Self.

Prepare for the Easter celebration, as a member of this generation on planet Earth, shifting from the separated human to the whole emerging Universal Human. During Easter, we enter into the wedding day of our Self, our Essential Self, with our Universal Self.

THERE IS NO CONTRADICTION BETWEEN OUR PERSONAL NEEDS AND EVOLUTIONARY NEEDS

Easter Day. The day of resurrection. That is a day after crucifixion because:

- Who among us has not experienced crucifixion?
- Who among us has not experienced being misunderstood, being misrecognized?
- Who among us has not felt the experience of betrayal?

We can only be betrayed by people who could never betray us. And yet, we don't stay in betrayal. We move beyond the *tragic* of betrayal to the *post-tragic* of resurrection. We enter into the field of prayer.

We are here in Bethlehem together. We are bearers of the good news, and we are the good news ourselves. The message is us. We are messengers who forgot their message.

We *are* the message. We *are* the new humans. *Homo amor.*

We are committed to birthing the new human in each of us and with it the new humanity. Because it is *only* that kind of sea change—that kind of fundamental transformation of identity that was brought about by the likes of the Renaissance—that can respond to the existential risk that threatens our very survival in this moment in time.

Paradoxically, when we speak of existential risk:

- We do not need to contract.
- We do not need to close our hearts.
- We do not need to feel that the gap between our ability to feel the pain and heal the pain is too great, and in that gap we close our hearts.

No, it is quite the opposite.

In that realization of genuine existential risk:

- We embrace the joy of our calling.
- We embrace the joy of being an Evolutionary Unique Self resonating with the unique evolutionary impulse that lives in us.

We respond to the unique need in our unique circle of intimacy and influence. By giving the unique gift that is only ours to give and speaking our voice into the Unique Self Symphony, we are being not *power-less* but *em-powered*.

When we resonate the code, we are *doing resonance,* as a verb—we are talking about how we have a unique gift to give to the unique need of Reality at this moment in time.

But what of my needs? How do my personal needs address, intersect with, or interpenetrate the need of Reality? What is the relationship between personal needs and evolutionary needs?

PERSONAL NEEDS MEET OUR EVOLUTIONARY NEEDS

Addressing and saying my personal need—at this very moment in real time—does not contradict the need to do prayer at this moment.

Often, people will pray only for world peace, which is so beautiful.

How gorgeous to expand our consciousness and genuinely pray for world peace! But what we always say together is: **we can never bypass our personal needs.**

We can never bypass.

> *Prayer affirms the dignity of personal need. Our personal needs always meet our evolutionary needs.*

There is ultimately no contradiction between them, but we have to begin with affirming the dignity of our personal need. As the great master of the Hasidic movement, the Baal Shem Tov said, when he spoke to his friends, *When you pray, ask for everything!*

Ask for everything: Oh my god! My uncle, my brother, my friend. I pray that I can make a living and that I can find my voice. I pray I can be healed of this particular physical ailment, or I can learn to live with this ailment—my back pain—or could I find a new drug for it? We ask for everything.

When we bypass our personal needs, we are heretics because we are committing heresy against the very nature of Reality, which structured our very essence as beings that need.

Do we need to distinguish between our authentic needs and our pseudo-needs?

Of course, we need to distinguish between our authentic and our pseudo-needs, and although we are so often shamed for our needs, we must know that need is holy, and need is real.

Why do we love babies? Because babies embrace their needs. There is no split between a baby and the baby's needs. As we get older:

- We begin to disown our core needs.
- We are shamed for our needs.
- We are humiliated for our needs.

We need to reclaim, in prayer, the dignity of our personal need and to know that the Divine—the god we don't believe in doesn't exist—the Divine that is the insistent and incessant creativity of All-That-Is, and the **Divine that created us with needs, affirms the dignity of our need**, and sits with us and loves with us, in *our holy and our broken Hallelujah*.

We all need each other. It's fundamental.

It's *a cold and a broken Hallelujah*. We offer it up. We come together for the sake of All-That-Is. At this time of intense crisis, as we always say, *crisis is an evolutionary driver; crisis opens up transformation*. Oh my God! Oh my Goddess!

We're creating it together. It's spontaneous. It's emergent.

> *We are the Unique Self Symphony arising in prayer and activism to demand from all of us that we awaken as Outrageous Lovers and that we respond to the outrageous pain of the world with Outrageous Love.*

We offer prayers. We have the dignity and delight of feeling and praying. We don't skip personal needs. Shout the prayers. All the gates are open. We can all get in.

I am praying for everything: light, love, money, health, peace, joy, and light.

We serve and fulfill our mission to the Creator and creation in the fullness of truth.

How do personal needs meet our evolutionary needs? How does it all become one? Feel the utter joy in the dignity of personal need.

OUR EMERGENCE AS AN EVOLUTIONARY HUMAN

What does the resurrection of Christ mean to us in fulfilling a personal need?

Personal need means expressing the full divine potential of the evolutionary process with others and to awaken to a planet filled with love. We have a personal need, but *not only* for our own comfort and well-being. **Our own comfort and well-being depend on having an open-endedness for our Universal Self and *Homo universalis*—the new species—as we undoubtedly enter a universe filled with life.**

Let's see how the resurrection possibly went. I'll tell a story here. In 1980, I (Barbara) was in Santa Barbara writing a book on the future human and the new human. I saw hang gliders coming off a cliff and jumping above a cross at Mount Calvary monastery. *Because the hang gliders had butterfly-colored delta wings, I got the image of mass metamorphosis.* I got that the meaning of the resurrection was to demonstrate that the person is going to be transformed. Jesus did not come back as a cosmic spirit. He came back as a new *being* in the story.

That is what Mary Magdalene saw—this new being was imbued with Spirit to such a degree that he could materialize and dematerialize. Every religion has had a vision of that kind of capability. It appears to be imminent in the human species.

When you love God above all else, you are nature as yourself; you are the nature of the entire Universe as an expression of yourself and others.

Love others as yourself and combine it with science and technology, and you will all be changed—in a moment—in the twinkling of an eye.

Evolutionary Christ came in very early in time to demonstrate to our entire species that when we combine love, creativity, science, and technology, the whole universe moves towards our emergence as an *evolutionary human*, a new human.

If we take the words *new human* the whole way, this new human would incarnate Christ *Consciousness* in bodies ever more sensitive to thought.

When I was having my Christ experience, I said to this presence, what shall I call you? The presence said, call me your "Potential Self"—I am here to inform you that *that's who you are.*

It was impossible to believe that until very recently. Now, I can imagine the other side of the existential crisis.

Let's look at the crisis of devolution and destruction, the existential crisis, and let's look at the existential opportunity. That is the other side of the existential crisis.

Let's *project* ourselves fifty years if we do not self-destruct sooner. Let's say we make it through this crisis.

Can you imagine:

- The human who is able to experience that inner Unique Self as who we are, becoming an Evolutionary Unique Self joining with other Evolutionary Unique Selves imbued with that impulse?
- Our bodies becoming ever more sensitive to thought—extending our life, extending our consciousness, extending our creativity?
- Us in fifty years, crossing the threshold to say, I am *Homo universalis*. I had been *Homo sapiens sapiens*.

I have not been Neanderthal or *Homo habilis* or *Homo erectus*. They are all gone. *Homo sapiens* is still here. It's clear to me what the need of the evolutionary *Homo sapiens* is.

The need is to become one with that higher essence of our own being, in love, in creativity, in action, and to create a world equal to our potential. And as we come to mass resonance on this planet, knowing that we are not alone.

The ultimate purpose is a planetary awakening in love through Unique Self Symphonies.

That would mean the entire planetary body is awakening—in the consciousnesses of those who are already awakening. We are already here. It's not like it's going to be something that nobody has ever known. It is all here, but it's never been together.

Awakening is occurring through a Unique Self Symphony, each one of us sounding a unique note. **Maybe it's a jazz symphony—in the sense that we begin to play with each other within the symphony**. The essence of how we tap into the self-organizing Universe is by joining with each other in creativity that is self-organizing out of love.

In other words, we become the Universe evolving through the Unique Self Symphony, aiming at a planetary awakening in love. This would be the Teilhard de Chardin vision of the noosphere—*the thinking layer of Earth*—infused with all of us getting its collective eyes.

Back to the code:

You are entering an extended wedding day of the Essential Self and the Universal Self. This is the marriage of your evolving human self and your Universal Self.

This is the point of contact that allows the Universal Self to infuse you, as a human being, with its power and glorious radiance towards the resurrection of humanity, towards the fulfillment of a planet awakening in love, as experience merges with your Universal Self, the highest frequency of your being.

This vibration stimulates joy and ecstasy, leading to the union of the earthly human with its Universal Self. It is a gradual and progressive process.

The Universal Self feels like an angel embracing and infusing you with its frequency, so that there is no separation among the levels within yourself. The inner cacophony becomes harmonized as the Universe Self's frequency calibrates all the lesser frequencies.

Let us celebrate, on the Easter weekend, in this great moment of planetary transition, the emergence of our Universal Selves and a planet awakening in love, with each of our notes, each of our genius codes, each of our brilliance:

- Joining with our beloved, our lovers, wherever they may be
- Joining with each other, lovers all, for the planetary awakening
- In Christian language, this would be *a second coming of the Christ*

WE MUST MEET OUR SIX CORE ESSENTIAL NEEDS

Easter has been honored in this moment, and in such a beautiful and evolutionary way—that Easter has never been seen before. Easter has been resurrected at a higher level of consciousness.

We look at each other, and we say, *what does love mean?* Is it ordinary love that is a strategy of ego and security? Is that our need?

Or, do we have the following core needs?

- To feel recognized
- To feel desired
- To feel chosen
- To feel adored
- To feel recognized
- To feel intended

Those are the six core human needs. I want to say them again.

We have a desire but not just a desire of the ego, not just ordinary love, not just to get over our discomfort and insecurity.

Our deepest desire is to have our needs met.

We are affirming the dignity of personal need because our deepest need is our evolutionary need. We are going to see how they merge together. We are going to see what it means to affirm the *six core human needs*. They are:

I need to be intended. That is why people love when someone intends an anniversary present or birthday wishes. When they plan it beforehand, and it's not spontaneous, I feel intended. I feel your intention in your attention.

Then, I realize Reality itself intended me. I don't just need the intention of that other separate self who is beautiful, who mediates Reality's intention. I need to know Reality and Source intended me. That is the truth because that's what it means to be a Unique Self—to know your uniqueness is to know Reality intended you.

Then, I need to know that I am desired. But, I am not just desired by the person next to me, who happens to desire me. We have exiled desire to human desire, and sexual desire, and to a particular kind of human sexual desire—the way a 21-year-old feels about a 19-year-old. That is where all of desire goes. No! I am desired by Reality. **Reality desires me because Reality manifested me utterly uniquely.**

Yes, I desire to be chosen, but not by someone who happens to pass by and we have some mutual sense of brokenness that can be healed in hanging out together so that we can cover up the brokenness. No!

I am chosen by Reality. Reality chose us and that is manifest in our uniqueness. Reality chooses me.

All of a sudden, we get it! Reality intended me. Reality desires me. Reality chooses me.

Then I have a desire to be recognized because we are all systematically misrecognized. So, we desperately search for someone to recognize us until we realize, *Oh my God, that need to be recognized—Reality recognizes me, and that is why I am unique.* **I am utterly unique and distinct. That is the recognition of Reality.**

I need to be adored, and then I realize, *oh my God, Reality adores me.* I have an utterly dazzlingly beautiful unique cellular structure, molecular structure, and subatomic structure that took Reality billions of years to manifest. Imagine if someone spends millions of years in a garage making you a perfect present, which is a portrait of you. Wouldn't I know that I am adored? Reality adores me.

My sixth need is a big one. Reality needs me. I am needed. I have a need to be needed.

Wow! What are my needs, my friends?

- I have a need to be intended.
- I have a need to be desired.
- I have a need to be chosen.
- I have a need to be recognized.
- I have a need to be adored.
- I have a need to be needed.

Those are my core essential needs. Here is what we call in *tantra* the deep principle of tracing things back to their roots.

Everyone thinks tantra is about sexuality, but one percent of tantra text talks about sexuality.

Sexuality is a model for life. You can be erotic and celibate. Eros dripping Eros. It's about living an erotic life. Living an erotic life is living a life, pulsating, creating, and experiencing all of your needs met. Giving your pulsating gorgeous gift and imprinting that kiss on the lips of Reality.

That is what it is all about. Let's feel so deeply. Every one of our personal needs can be traced back, at its core, to one of these six needs.

I want to be healthy so I can feel my joy. When I feel my joy, I can feel my radical aliveness and give my gifts. That is why I don't want to be healthy to be healthy. I want to be healthy because I am needed in the world. I want to be healthy in order to survive. **I want to survive because I realize in some deep place that I am needed.** I am not extra because I have something to say and something to do.

Always trace your needs back to their roots.

If you trace your need back to its root, you will realize that every small need is part of a larger need. But you cannot bypass the small need.

You can't say, I am not going to be healthy.

We are going to embrace our physicality and take better care of our bodies, affirming the dignity of what our bodies needed in terms of food and exercise.

All of our needs!

My need to be adored.
My need to be desired.
My need to be needed.
My need to be intended.
My need to be recognized.
My need to be chosen.

Those are sacred needs of Reality. The only deep transformative tantric *holy trick* is what spiritual practices are about. **Transmute those needs and realize they cannot be filled by someone who just passes by**, who is broken, like I am broken, and it seems they are going to fill those needs for me, so I make them the sole repository of all those needs and believe that they are the source of all my resources.

No.

In order to get true resources, I've got to go back to Source and realize Reality needs me. Reality adores me. Reality chooses me. Reality intends me. Reality recognizes me. Reality desires me. Oh my god!

Know that love is not ordinary love. It is Outrageous Love, in which I know that my need is the need of Reality. No need is extra, and no need is bypassed. Let's open it up! Let's rip our hearts open in surrender before the depth of our power. Let's pray together. "I Want to Know What Love Is," Foreigner [*See Appendix*]

How do I bring together personal need and evolutionary need and know that my needs matter?

It is only by meeting my needs and affirming their dignity, their glory, their beauty that I can meet the needs of all of Reality rising in me.

OUR TRUE NEED IS TO PLAY A LARGER GAME

Here is an Easter thought about our evolutionary needs: **We really need to become evolutionary humans.** We are born at this shift point. No matter whether the need is to be needed, to be loved, to be appreciated, to have your physical needs met, *all of that*.

All of that is really only part of this thrust, this huge impulse in the *Evolutionary Human*, particularly, for union of the Divine, as co-creators of a new world, a new consciousness, a new life.

We get to evolutionary need not the way the communists did, who did the first version of evolutionary spirituality, and who bypassed human needs.

What we are saying is—my need to be intended by another, to be desired, to be chosen, to be recognized, to be adored, and to be needed—those can't be fulfilled by somebody else adoring me. **They can't be fulfilled by somebody else needing me**. They can't be fulfilled that way.

I've got to realize that Reality intended me and needs my evolutionary partnership.

That Reality desires me and needs my union.

That Reality recognizes me.

That Reality adores me. That all of life is to evolve and realize my true need.

My true need is to play a larger game. I want to play a larger game. I want to participate in the evolution of love.

When we say *Reality*, we are saying *God*.

God needs me.

God created me to be an expression of God.

That is why the *confessions of greatness* are necessary. When I think of God needing us, then I do have some opinion as to the purpose of God: to create humans in the image of God or co-creators, God is creating co-creators to express that love of God in individual and free humans. That is the great intention of Reality.

Since that has been going for 13.8 billion years, there is a lot of force going with it.

So, when we say, Reality intended me, desires me, chooses me, recognizes me, adores me, and needs me, what we are saying is—in the language of the great evolutionary mystics:

- God needs your service.
- God desires your service.
- God desires and needs your partnership.
- God desires and needs your pleasure.

There is a beautiful text that says that we are held accountable in judgment for every pleasure we haven't experienced in the world.

That doesn't just mean that we walk into Baskin-Robbins and they say, you missed three flavors! Oh my God, you missed three flavors. I can't believe you sinner. You missed three flavors in Baskin-Robbins! Send them down to hell!

No, it means something so much deeper.

I have to up-level my pleasure, and the highest pleasure is to respond to the divine need, to respond to the evolutionary need.

There is no greater pleasure than to know that we have greatness that is uniquely needed by All-That-Is.

"How Could Anyone?" Libby Roderick [*See Appendix*]

Find the song and sing it out loud! Know that we need each other. It's the glory. We are not codependent. We are an evolutionary family enacting a Unique Self Symphony.

I (Marc) need Barbara Marx Hubbard. What a delight to say that out loud.

Wow! We need each other. We need each other in family. Confess your greatness. What are you taking a stand for in the world?

It is us, it is we, it is our unique we. Let us speak our greatness. Let our voices into the noosphere.

The noosphere is the beautiful mind, heart, and body of God that is Reality.

When we confess our greatness, the Source within us is the Source we are confessing. So it is really expressing the greatness of God as you.

We seek to connect with all great faiths when they see their unique potential to the whole.

CHAPTER SIX

EVOLUTION IS LOVE IN ACTION

Episode 26 — April 22, 2017

ATTUNING TO YOUR UNIQUE GIFTS IN THE SYMPHONY

How do your needs fit into the Unique Self Symphony? We may never have asked ourselves that question, but let's feel what it will be like.

Get in touch with the time when you feel you fit best, when somebody else was giving their gift and you were giving yours, and there was a feeling of excitement, of joy, and you entered what we call a WeSpace within the Unique Self Symphony.

Get in touch with a time when you felt you fit best into something greater than the sum of your parts. When there were others there, when you felt *we* were fitting best.

This is a new word we've invented—*symphonize*. **You are actually attuning your unique gifts with others in the Unique Self Symphony**, and what happens when you do that? Well, you play a little jazz.

Pick somebody, and play a little jazz with that person. Play a unique back and forth, each instrument more than it was:

- You are no longer alone.

- You are fitting into the Unique Self Symphony.
- You are creating something radically new.
- You have joined the self-creating universe, consciously.
- You have joined within the Unique Self Symphony to harmonize—and to fulfill that uniqueness that cannot be filled without being part of the #WeSpace—towards a planetary awakening in love.

We are the planet awakening in love. We are resonating with each other as each of us gives our impulse into the world, with all others yearning to do the same.

ARE YOU NEEDED BY THE UNIQUE SELF SYMPHONY, OR ARE WE JUST MAKING IT UP?

We are talking about Unique Self Symphony, not just as a symphony where you are playing the notes that were already written—although you are playing them uniquely and beautifully—but what we are calling a **Unique Self *jazz* Symphony; as we come together, we create new moments and new movements that never were before**.

We realize that in us coming together as Evolutionary Unique Selves, in order to lay down a new politics of Evolutionary Love—as an act of activism and transformation, as our response to the existential risk that challenges and threatens our planet—we respond with an affirmation of life by evolving intimacy and introducing a new movement, a new jazz movement in the great Unique Self Symphony.

The jazz movement in the Unique Self Symphony is precisely the idea of the Unique Self Symphony as the next iteration of evolution.

We come together bottom-up, not top-down, and evolve possibility and respond to existential risk.

Can you feel this?

Are you needed by the Unique Self Symphony?

Is your instrument needed to create this jazz, or are we just making this up?

We live in a world of outrageous pain, and the only response to outrageous pain is Outrageous Love. We look at each other and love each other outrageously—as the source of creation, of evolution, that lives in us.

How can anyone ever tell us that our love is less than beautiful? And how deeply we are connected in our souls!

PRAYER IS A REALIZATION OF THE INTIMATE UNIVERSE

Prayer affirms the dignity of personal need.

Do we pray to Santa Claus? I happen to like Santa Claus.

I do believe in fairies, but we do not pray to Santa Claus.

We pray to the quality of the Divine which is the Infinity of Intimacy.

We live in an Intimate Universe. The best evolutionary science, the best chaos theory, complexity theory, the best interior sciences, reveal and disclose the Intimate Universe.

Everything is interconnected, and the interior of interconnectivity is intimacy.

Therefore, Isaiah cries out 2,000 years ago, and evolutionary science reveals some of the structures today. Isaiah cries out in the name of the Infinity of Intimacy, *imo anochi b'tzarah*: I am with you in your pain, and I am with you in your joy.

We may live lives, sometimes, of quiet desperation, but we never live lives of lonely desperation because every place we fall, we fall into God/Goddess' hands, and that is not an image. It is not a fantasy; it is the fact of Reality.

- It is not a belief.
- It is not a dogma.
- It is a *realization*.

It is the realization of what we call the second person of God.

It is the realization of God as the Infinity of Intimacy.

When we love each other—and we feel that personal quality of intimacy between us—we realize that our intimacy participates in the Infinity of Intimacy. When we come before God, we come as both God's partner and as those that are held by God. And God says, *I am holding you, and whenever you fall, you fall into my hand.*

WHO ARE YOU? THE UNIQUE SELF RESPONSE

You are an irreducible, unique expression of the LoveIntelligence and LoveBeauty, that is the initiating and animating energy and Eros of All-That-Is, that lives in you, as you, and through you, that never was is or will be ever again, other than through you.

And as such you have an irreducible, unique perspective and your unique perspective, plus your unique quality of intimacy plus your unique presence, plus your unique taste make up your Unique Self.

And your Unique Self has a unique gift to give to your unique circle of intimacy and influence that addresses a unique need that can be addressed, ever and only, by you.

As such, you stand on the abyss of darkness, and you say, with your unique singular frequency of light, *let there be light!*

And you address a corner of the world that is unloved, until that unique expression of LoveIntelligence, that is the evolutionary impulse awakening as you, is exploded into the world through your love.

That is the answer to the question, "Who are you"?

With that confession of greatness, we go into our psalm, "Hallelujah," the holy and the broken *Hallelujah*, which is the confession of our vulnerability.

We confess our greatness, and we confess our vulnerability, and then we bring it and lay it on the altar of the Mother—in prayer.

Hallelujah! We offer our personal need; we confess our vulnerability. We confess our vulnerability from the place of our confession of greatness. We offer up our holy and our broken *Hallelujah*, and we pray for our personal needs because prayer affirms the dignity of personal need.

Do not wait for other people to do it. *We are not spectators while other people offer their prayers.* Let's open up all the gates!

I pray for my uncle who has cancer who has surgery this week.

I confess my vulnerability. I don't sit back, just lost in some egoic construction of greatness. I offer my full vulnerability.

Friends! All the gates are open! **We cannot find our greatness unless we find our vulnerability.**

We can fall like children before the Divine, before the Infinity of Intimacy, before the LoveIntelligence of Reality that manifested photosynthesis way before there were human beings, and that holds us in every second.

We break open our vulnerability. We offer up our prayer, and it is in the purity of the prayer, that the gates open.

Bring it together. Personal need. Our own vulnerability. Prayer affirms the dignity of personal need, and our personal need matters before the Divine. The infinity of all the laws of physics looks at us and holds us. All of the infinite cosmic years and light years and all the infinite laws of the universe are sitting in the chair in front of me, knowing me, holding me, and caring about every detail of my life. Everything that moves through us, the whole story. Our prayers are lifted up all the way into the deepest place on the Inside of the Inside.

We turn our prayers into a message; we turn our prayers into *dharma*, as we raise up *prayer as activism*.

PLANET EARTH IS GIVING BIRTH TO A CO-EVOLVING HUMANITY

We are celebrating the planetary birthday through a Unique Self Symphony that is connecting billions of us through our Unique Self.

Prayer for our individual needs extends into our prayer for planetary expression because every one of us, to meet even one personal need, needs to go further to let that personal go the whole way to express that full potential self that wants to connect with others. **We are uniting the personal, the transpersonal, and the evolutionary, in giving everything**, just like in that beautiful music, "Hallelujah."

Literally the birth, through each one of us and to us collectively, reveals for the very first time on Earth the enormity of the potentiality of planet Earth giving birth to its full potential, through every one of us.

This is not an illusion; this is not something we are just making up in a workshop. This is the direction of evolution.

Mother Earth is giving birth to a new humanity who is able to carry the fulfillment of Earth to the next stage. This is the planetary awakening, to celebrate the planetary birth of the awakening potential, not only of us as individuals, but us *collectively*.

The genius of Mother Earth herself, struggling in this very moment with existential destruction, is at the very same time awakening to existential

Reality. This is like a mother giving birth to a child. Birth is painful. The baby does not like it; it hurts. And then something starts to come through, and it is a new organism, a new being.

Imagine everything we know how to do and be and give, working toward a planetary awakening in love. Make it real. We call upon each Unique Self as a microcosm of every Unique Self on planet Earth.

Every one of us is truly an expression of uniqueness. But let's feel ourselves connected to anyone, anywhere on Earth, who would like to give their gift to the whole for the Unique Self Symphony.

- Feel the talent.
- Feel the innovation.
- Feel the creativity.
- Feel the goodness.

Feel the technological genius orchestrating naturally, to celebrate what everybody wants to give in order to feel completely needed in the planetary awakening! It's the fulfillment of the heart's desire of the human species.

> *Can you imagine having as our purpose the fulfillment of the deepest longing and heart's desire of each person on Earth to give their gift fully into a field great enough to receive them?*

And having this result in a planetary awakening in love?

Awaken the species. Let's believe in this actual possibility of a planetary awakening. When this happens, mass resonance will be created on planet Earth.

It would be like just after a baby's birth, while it is crying, upset, and does not like it...

It is held in its mother's arms, and what happens is, its nervous system relaxes.

It opens its eyes and smiles, taking its first breath.

It smiles; it is not alone; it is coming home.

Somebody is orchestrating this from a very high level of planetary, internet, noosphere contact, and we all have a shared experience:

- We are one.
- We are whole.
- We are co-creative with the divine process of evolution.
- We are being born as the universal species.

On this Earth and in the Universe beyond, we are sending out the signal from Mother Earth that her goal, all along, has been to give birth to a co-evolving, co-creative humanity.

We are the exact generation when this is happening.

We are called together to create an experience of awakening for our planet in love.

With this declaration, not only do we overcome a sense of loneliness by becoming part of the Unique Self Symphony, but we enter into a moment of deep, deep fulfillment of desire, a deep, joyful fulfillment of the passion to express our greatness.

The Isaiah prayer is the prayer of the actualization of the experience in the present to bring it through. It's not praying for something to happen some other time; it's a prayer of experiencing a planetary awakening together.

Tune into how it feels to call for the awakening, in a communion of visionary souls, reaching worldwide to people in every culture, every religion, and every place on this Earth, in this frequency.

Let's use that internal frequency of the Unique Self Symphony to orchestrate ourselves and conclude with a *Hallelujah!*

Planet Earth is giving birth to a co-evolving, co-creative humanity.

Thank you, God.

THE INTIMATE UNIVERSE IS A SYNERGISTIC UNIVERSE

We symphonize. With no words that cannot be spoken, we are calling forth the vision together, the great new vision of a planetary awakening in love through Unique Self Symphonies.

That vision is not the old messianic vision in which the man will come riding on the white donkey and announce the *Messiah*, and we will flock to them.

We *participate* in this new vision of *Messiah*. We *are* the music. The vision can't happen—the music can't happen—without us playing our instrument.

That's the whole story.

This planetary awakening in love through Unique Self Symphonies all over the world, in which we enact a self-organizing Universe drawn by the strange attractor of every human being knowing:

- I am needed by All-That-Is.
- I have a gift to give.
- I am a Unique Self.

And what is a Unique Self? What is the Unique Self equation?

> *Unique Self = your unique perspective + your unique quality of intimacy + your unique presence + your unique taste*

Your Unique Self has a unique gift to give, which is your instrument in the symphony that addresses a unique need in your unique circle of intimacy and influence that can be addressed by no one that ever was, is, or will be other than you.

Imagine the mass resonance enacted through a technologically interconnected planet, as a symphony.

Symphony is synergy.

The Intimate Universe is a synergistic Universe in which the parts come together to express a whole greater than the sum of the parts, which is the new vision, the evolution of intimacy.

Reality is not a fact; it is a story. And evolution means that it is a story, but it is not a theory *out there*, it is a theory *in here*. Evolution is not a fact out there; we are *personally implicated*. Evolution awakens in us as a unique intimate instrument of that symphony, and Reality needs our service.

GOD NEEDS US

Complete the sentence: God needs me to...

When we say God, we always say: the god you don't believe in doesn't exist.

God is the God who is the incessant, ceaseless creativity of Cosmos, the self-organizing Universe, which is also the Infinity of Intimacy that knows your name.

God needs me to, what?

God needs us to have the audacity to be true to our truest heart.

Go the next step further: how should you spread love? *Spread love* is beautiful but too amorphic. We would love the New Age to open our hearts but *how?*

To make the Unique Self Symphony work, we have to move from New Age proclamation or declaration into something very specific. This is the note in the symphony.

You cannot join a symphony by saying, *I'm going to feel into how the violin feels*. When you play the violin in a symphony, what you do is you play precise notes on a violin, and you play them as uniquely as you.

When you get up and play your trumpet with Louis Armstrong in a Unique Self Jazz Symphony, you are not just playing your trumpet, but you are *in there*.

You are offering up everything, you are giving your specific unique gifts.

In order for a Unique Self Symphony to happen, we need to move from New Age intention, to this new human potential, claiming that these are the specific actions, the specific unique gifts, that we are going to give into our unique circle of intimacy and influence, that are real, specific, actionable, and accountable.

Can we realize that God needs us to do something that will only be done in the world if we do it?

We can't just get online and meditate together; it is not enough. That alone won't change the world, and it is why policymakers don't take the New Age seriously.

Let's have a mass resonance!

Let's actually enact love.

Evolution is love in action. Evolution is Spirit in action.

Our job is to comfort the afflicted—and we are all afflicted—but it is also to afflict the comfortable. And we are all a little comfortable.

God needs our service—*avodah tzorech gavoha*—Reality needs us. Meaning if we don't act, the action will not happen.

Nachman of Breslov, Marc's lineage master, said: the reason Reality created atheism is because, when it comes to committing your Outrageous Acts of Love, you need to be an atheist.

What does that mean? It means there is no one to do it but you. That is the point of the evolutionary impulse.

The evolutionary impulse says, *you are Messiah*. You are the expression of the Divine.

God holds us.

We fall into God's hands.

But can we transition out of this place where we declare, where we take upon ourselves and realize:

If Barbara and Marc do not do Evolutionary Church every week, it's not going to be done.

If Annika doesn't show up in the gorgeous way she does and get serious in this new career she's starting, so she can do the special learning spaces she wrote about, it is not going to happen.

Ninety-five percent of life is showing up and doing it for real.

Oh my God, *om namah Shivaya*. We greet the great Lord Shiva.

Our invitation is to realize, to really get in our body—not just in our heart, not just in our mind, but in our toenails: the resonance, the full awakening is through us.

That's our chant. That's our song.

With our own two hands, we are going to do the next thing, it is our action to do, and it's not going to happen in any other way.

There is exhortation in that. We have to move from New Age to new action. *New action* is global awakening, a resonance in love through Unique Self Symphonies.

CHAPTER SEVEN

REFLECTIONS ON *CONVERSATIONS WITH GOD* AND *OUTRAGEOUS LOVE*

Episode 27 — April 29, 2017

AWAKENING DHARMA: RESONANCE AND PLANETARY EVOLUTION

What is *dharma*? The wisdom, the knowledge, and the awareness that we are expressions of the whole process of evolution, internalized in a resonant field.

Activate the *dharma*, that uniqueness that is holding the code of your own evolution as you enter the Unique Self Symphony. It is your part of the symphony that is leading to a planetary awakening.

Let's be the planet awakening—every one of us. I am the planet awakening now. I'm on the internet, noosphere, nervous system of humanity now. Every second.

Every breath in the Evolutionary Church is contributing to the planetary awakening, and what this does is it makes every instant potent with power that is true.

We are with Neale Donald Walsch whose book series, *Conversations With God*, has spread throughout the world, giving people the awareness that they are in conversations with God already.

Imagine a conversation with ourselves as a highly evolved species. We are going to awaken the species in ourselves, not only the planetary awakening in this moment but us awakening to awareness of highly evolved beings throughout the Universe and within ourselves. Feel it with your attention, manifesting within you. We are all here now.

FROM BROKEN HALLELUJAH TO EVOLUTIONARY DHARMA: RECLAIMING THE DIVINE

What is Evolutionary Church about? It is about up-leveling the whole story—that the god you do not believe in does not exist. So, here's an image as we move towards prayer.

"Battle Hymn of the Republic," Julia Ward Howe [*See Appendix*]

You might wonder why we have switched from that to Leonard Cohen's "Hallelujah." Both songs have *Hallelujah, glory, glory, Hallelujah. His truth is marching on.*

There is something really beautiful about that and something really scary about it. Okay, something really beautiful and something really scary.

In the story of *Hallelujah* in "Mine Eyes Have Seen the Glory" (a civil war song), *he hath loosed the fateful lightning*—it is an angry god. It is a dogma god. It is a god who is the only exclusive truth. At the time that that song was written, the Christians thought that they had exclusive truth. The Muslims and other parts of the world thought they had the exclusive truth, and the Jews of course. No, maybe it is the Tibetan Buddhists. We are not sure. But everyone has exclusive truths, and everyone has god on their side.

His truth is marching on means: "my truth goes marching on." Feuerbach[13] said, *I have projected onto god in order to protect myself.* Hallelujah also means pristine praise, or *hallelut*. This kind of ecstasy and the outbreath of God is hijacked. The church has been hijacked by various forms of fundamentalist dogma.

Now, Leonard Cohen comes and says, *Hallelujah*, but in this *Hallelujah* is all of my uncertainty, and it is my holy *Hallelujah*, and it is my broken *Hallelujah*.

It is not all clear, and it is not a song of someone who says, *I have seen the light, I can hold all the uncertainty, and I can live in the uncertainty.* Now this is really important. **We actually need both. Leonard Cohen's "Hallelujah" has just one piece of the story.**

It is:

> The glory of our finitude,
> The glory of our poignancy,
> The glory of our brokenness,
> The glory of us being on our knees

Whenever we're on our knees, we are on our knees before God—and it's gorgeous.

But we also need to reclaim our holy certainties—not certainties of dogma but as certainties of *dharma*. By *dharma*, we mean:

- The good news, or evangelism
- The good news that the Universe is a love story
- The good news that the Universe is allurement, all the way up and all the way down
- The good news of conscious evolution

---

13 Ludwig Andreas Feuerbach (1804–1872) was a German philosopher best known for his critical analysis of religion and his contributions to materialist and humanist philosophy. Feuerbach is considered an important figure in the transition from German idealism to modern materialism and atheism.

- The good news that we are Outrageous Lovers, unique expressions of the LoveIntelligence of the Cosmos
- The good news of the confessions of our greatness

It is not that it is all uncertainty. **It is not that we know nothing; we have exploded dogma, and we move into *dharma*, and we come before God in prayer.** So, let's bring our *Hallelujah,* the *Hallelujah* of Leonard Cohen, but let's bring with it our vision, purpose, and direction as we step in this week welcoming Neale Donald Walsch.

We are so delighted and honored to be here with you.

Amen. *Hallelujah.*

We let go of our exclusive god, and we embrace the broken *Hallelujah.*

As we say our hymn, "Mine Eyes Have Seen the Glory," even as we speak this new truth with holy audacity, we come before God, and we confess our vulnerability—we cannot do it all ourselves.

We are children, and we fall before God—not the god we don't believe in, who doesn't exist—but God who is the Infinity of Intimacy.

God who is all of the **third person,** the laws of physics and chemistry, the infinite, gorgeousness of Cosmos, dazzling complexity, the light years, everything.

We participate in the intimacy of that gorgeous, exponentially powerful God who is not just the Infinity of Power but also the Infinity of Intimacy that knows our name and God in the **second person,** the God that Rumi spoke of: *Let me fall into the arms of the Beloved, and whenever I fall, I fall into Her hands.*

And so, when we pray, we ask for everything. We come before God, and we say, *God, help me really know who I am.*

God is the Infinity of Intimacy, and we are going to free the Divine from the grist, the grasp, of fundamentalism; we offer a hijack of the fundamental, personal god.

Let's go and feel the power of prayer, feel the gorgeousness, then go the next step and not just confess our vulnerability; we are going to confess our greatness.

CONFESSIONS OF GREATNESS FOR PLANETARY AWAKENING

I (Barbara) first understood this one day when I was expressing gratitude to God. I said:

> thank you God for this;
> thank you God for that;
> thank you for all the beauty…

Then I heard a voice saying, *thank you, Barbara*, and I realized that what God was saying was that the God in me was Him/Her/It becoming god-like.

What God was pleased about was to hear God-in-me speaking Itself and Its greatness.

God placed uniqueness and greatness of evolutionary intelligence into everyone. So confessing our greatness is really thanking God for indwelling in us, as us. Could there be a greater opportunity to say *thank you God* for the greatness of God within us?

Let's reclaim church, but let's claim it at a higher resonance. I confess:

I am a great being.

I can give this particular unique gift.

I have whatever gift it is to give which is gorgeous, unique, and beautiful.

I am an amazing lover.

We can actually confess our greatness. We used to confess our sin: *I am broken;* we confess our vulnerability. That is important, but now we want to confess our greatness. I confess:

> To the greatness of my transformative powers.
> That I feel love for all, each day.
> My creation of You as me.
> To me as an aspect of our divine light.
> That I feel love for all of us every day.
> I am an amazing hugger and laugher.
> That my abilities are great and sought after for the work of good, for love to be shown.
> I hold back Your gifts. I am sorry, please keep trying—I am just playing hard to get.
> I am nothing without You.
> I spread joy and humor.
> That my love is as big as the sky.

We confess the God within, and by confessing it, God and we are one at a level of joined genius. **We've talked about joining genius with each other, but when we confess the greatness of God within us, whose genius are we joining with? It's the genius of the Divine within me.** God is very pleased with that.

These confessions change everything, and our intention in confession is to evolve the entire institution of what church, synagogue, and mosque is. If human beings begin to confess their greatness and we participate together in a planetary awakening in love through Unique Self Symphonies—as hundreds of thousands of people come together through Evolutionary Church and Evolutionary Churches spread around the world—then we are articulating a politics of Evolutionary Love, a politics of Outrageous Love—not ordinary love but Outrageous Love.

Then something begins to happen. What is happening is the evolution of the person that I am, and you are, into co-creators. It has taken 13.7 billion years of effort to create individual beings capable of co-creating with the Creator within. So this is the emerging humanity being born in our midst in this church.

WE GET TO FALL IN LOVE AGAIN AND AGAIN

Let's sing together and look at each other so deeply in the eye—so deep, so beautiful, so holy. We thank Libby Roderick for the lyrics to this song. "How Could Anyone," Libby Roderick [*See Appendix*]

If you are with someone, turn to the person next to you, and sing it to them.

Sing it to the deep Divine within.
Sing it to the person next door.
Sing it to the teller at the bank.

We get to fall in love again and again. We have exiled falling in love to romance and to sexuality, as beautiful as those are. **We fall in love with everyone. To fall in love is to see with God's eyes.**

WELCOMING NEALE DONALD WALSCH: CONVERSATIONS WITH GOD WITHIN

Barbara

Hello Neale Donald Walsch, and welcome.

I want to just remember how I first met Neale. It was the night of Princess Diana's death, and I received a call from you that day out of the blue, and you said, *Hello Barbara. This is Neale Donald Walsch. I was wondering how I could help you.* I thought, how could Neale Donald Walsch help me?

We have just been praising God and giving thanks to the greatness within us, and I think of Neale as being the greatness of God within every one of us. I introduce Neale in that light because it seems from all your marvelous books, *Conversations With God,* that you have been getting the information from God that:

God is within us is.

God's greatness is what God is expecting of us.

We are all great.

I also want to introduce Neale in terms of the new book, *Awaken the Species,* and thank you for being willing to undertake that relationship with us—to normalize it rather than making it extreme.

In order to set our context, I share that this Evolutionary Church is dedicated to so much of what you are learning from conversations with God for the evolution of the human individual as a divine expression toward a planetary awakening in love.

So, Neale, would you give us a sense of what it might mean to be our first major guest?

FROM DOCTRINE TO DISCOVERY: AWAKENING THE SACRED WITHIN

Neale

What is the Evolutionary Church, and how does it relate to *Conversations With God*?

How could it relate to that?

I think that people all over the world are hungry for a way to congregate. We talk in churches of a congregation, and that is what a church is really. A true church is a congregation of people who are like-minded, like-willed, and created in the same image and likeness, which is the image and likeness of that which is Divinity itself; in my language, I call that God.

I think that churches are places where people congregate. What has happened in our world is:

There are fewer and fewer places people feel comfortable congregating anymore because some of the ideas that are being shared in those places, as sincerely as they are believed, and as deeply as they are shared from a place of love, are limited. The understandings, the awarenesses, that are shared in those places are limited.

I want to make something clear here: **I do not believe that all the world's religions are wrong**. I think that, obviously many, many, many of the teachings of the world's great religions have done a great deal of good in the world—they have changed people's lives. I do think that there is one systemic problem with the world's organized religions, and that is that those religions tend to be limited—that they are incomplete.

They are incomplete, and people who practice those religions feel to me like children who have learned how to add and subtract, and then think that is all there is to mathematics; when in fact, there is a great deal more to mathematics than that.

We are like children in that we have accepted the messages from our forebears and our forefathers, from thousands of years ago, and we have stopped exploring the question:

Is it possible that there is something more that we do not understand here, the understanding of which could change everything?

So what I observe the Evolutionary Church to be about, is giving people a new place to congregate; a place to gather once again and experience that sacred inner connection that we call congregation; to experience that connection without having to be burdened by so many of the messages that seem to be incomplete and not the total understanding and the total awareness to which we have now come to, and which we have now arrived at in largest measure, among an increasing number of the world's people.

It occurs to me that in the area of our most sacred beliefs, people are unwilling to do what we are willing to do in every other area of life.

We are willing to do it in science.

We are willing to do it in technology.

We are willing to do it in medicine.

But we are unwilling to do it in our most sacred beliefs; we are unwilling to question the prior assumptions in our understanding.

In our understandings of science, if we have a new scientific discovery, we question it immediately. The same thing is true in medicine. If we develop a new cure, we question it immediately. We put it to the test. The same thing is true in technology. **But in our ideas about religion, about our ideas about God, our ideas about our most sacred beliefs about life, and all of it in those areas, we tend to refuse to question the prior assumption.**

Therefore, we are moving even more deeply into the 21st century with understandings and beliefs from the first centruy, and before. If we did that in medicine, it would be like undertaking brain surgery with a sharp stick. It is not going to work. What we need to do is move into this next portion of our 21st century with the courage to explore the question.

Is it possible that there is something we do not fully understand here about God and about life—the understanding of which would change everything?

I believe there is. I believe that in the *Conversations With God* books, and many other books written by Barbara, Deepak, Marianne, Eckhart, Katie, and all the rest of us (and others we haven't even heard of yet), that the messages that are being sent forth by these sources, at least offer us a chance to explore, once again, the question we must never stop asking, the question God said to me in *Conversations with God*.

The answer is in the question itself. So we invite ourselves to ask that question: *Who are we in relationship to God?*

My answer to that question and the answer you'll find here at the Evolutionary Church is:
We are that. We are that. God said to us, *I am that I am.*

And what I say to God is, *I am that I am. I am that I am.* I humbly, with gratitude, and with deep sincerity, purity, and innocence—the innocence of the recently discovered—share with you my awareness: I am that. So are you.

When we move into the experience of being that, when we self-select, when we select ourselves to be among those who choose to be an example of what it means to express Divinity at the highest level that we are capable of, in as many of the moments as it becomes possible—**when we choose to be one of those who self-selects to do that, we position ourselves as being among those who can truly believe this, who can truly change the world.**

If somebody told me 25 years ago I was going to write a book that will be read by 15 million people and translated into 37 languages, I would have laughed in their face. But then I chose to accept the invitation to self-select, to be one of many millions of people around the world who have asked, *You know what? I have come here for a reason larger than what I can get out of it. I have come here for a reason of what I can put into it.*

Evolutionary Church is all about providing a platform for us to decide what it is we can put into this process that we call life itself, as an expression of our true identity, which is as a singularization of the Divine itself.

That is how it feels to me in answer to your question; this is the exact sermon that the Evolutionary Church gives.

Barbara

Amen. Hallelujah

Marc has brought forward the idea of the Universe as a love story—from the quarks being attracted to quarks, for allurement all the way up and all the way down, and I want you to know we are both listening here with the very deep ears of the Evolutionary Church.

What is your sense of our relationship with the highly evolved beings? And who are they?

HIGHLY EVOLVED BEINGS ARE PARTNERS IN HUMANITY'S TRANSMOGRIFICATION

Neale

First, let me make it clear that the dictations I took down were not conversations with highly evolved beings, and the book makes that very clear. If you're telling me now that I'm receiving this information from highly evolved beings, categorically, the answer was no—although you are continuing to have a conversation with God.

You see, here's where it starts to get very interesting. There's no difference between highly evolved beings and that which we call God. **There is no difference between us and that which we call God.**

So, in the highest sense, I am actually talking to myself.

But to speak in human terms and to use the words that human beings use trading back and forth, my answer to your question is that highly evolved beings are entities from another dimension, in my understanding, who are seeking to assist us, and whose relation in our own evolutionary process, and whose relationship with us, is as spiritual partners on the journey of evolution itself, not just spiritual partners with human beings here on Earth but spiritual partners with sentient beings on planets and in locations throughout the Cosmos.

It is incontrovertible. I don't think anyone could seriously doubt that there is intelligent life elsewhere in the Cosmos. Cosmologists and physicists now tell us that there is even more than one universe, that our universe is not the only universe, but in fact, our universe is one of a universe of universes. We do not live in a universe but rather in a multiverse, given that that is true.

There are billions and billions of stars and quadrillions and gazillions of planets revolving around those stars. **So for us to imagine that we are the only intelligent species in the Cosmos would be almost ridiculous and certainly arrogant.**

Obviously, there are other beings in the Cosmos, and some of them are far more evolved than we are. These are the beings that we are referring to as highly evolved beings. Some beings actually live in a different dimension, that is they can inter-dimensionally move from meta-physicality to physicality and back to meta-physicality, as I have been told in the book called *Conversations with God, Book Four: Awaken the Species*. It is the fourth book in the *Conversations with God* dialogue under that title, and it offers a chance to learn more about not just the existence of highly evolved beings from other dimensions, but what the difference is—because, of course, I asked God that question immediately.

Let's say that highly evolved beings are a given. Let's say that it is obvious that there is intelligent life elsewhere in the universe and probably some demonstrations of that life are more evolved than we are.

If that is true, I have to ask, *what is the difference*? What is the primary difference between highly evolved beings and human beings who are living in an unawakened state. God said, *I'll give you a list; you want a list I can give you?* I answered, *Please do*. So, God gave me a list of 16 major differences between beings who are existing in an awakened state and human beings who are still moving around in an unawakened state.

It is an extraordinary list that if we did nothing more than embrace some of the ideas into our daily lives, we would experience ourselves as highly evolved entities as well.

Our relationship, to answer your question directly, between us as humanity, as human beings and highly evolved beings, is that we are all one. They are part of who we are in the expanded sense that all sentient beings and all life in the universe is only one single thing. There is only one thing *Conversations with God* told us 20 years ago—all things are one thing. There is only one thing, and all things are part of the one thing we have an opportunity to utilize.

Even as my body now has ten fingers, I can ignore my ten fingers. I can ignore the other parts of myself, or I can use all the parts of myself—my eyes, my ears, and all the parts of myself—to expand my experience of self, and to notice and to express all that I truly am.

That is our relationship with highly evolved beings. They are telling us, *use us as the part of you that can express that which all of us know inherently is true* and that some of us have put into practice in our daily lives.

If you choose to do that, if you choose right now that you can make that shift, it is really a transmogrification. That's even higher than a transformation. We are not talking about transforming human beings anymore. We are talking about transmogrifying human beings.

Transmogrification is a shift in our ground of being, so surprising that it is almost magical.

A SACRED SECRET WITHIN US ALL

Barbara

You know, Neale, when I started to read and told people about your book, I said to them, I feel that I have personally been in touch with or connected with highly evolved beings, and that highly evolved beings had a specific message for me which was, "Barbara, you came to a 'stellar gate' knowing certain things that you couldn't talk about us because we wanted you to look normal."

I told some friends about this, and what happened was they all started to confess their relationship with highly evolved beings. These were pretty straightforward types, and they responded, *Oh really, well, this is what happened to me, and this is what happened to so-and-so.* I discovered many of us have these experiences but do not talk about them.

What is this relationship for all of us?

And I remember what you think about the relationship between us and maybe members of this church who are probably pretty sophisticated already in knowing that they are expressing the greatness of God as themselves.

NOT AN UNCOMMON DIALOGUE

[Neale]

It is what we create it to be. It is what we declare it to be. *I am.*

I am really not in a position, nor would I want to be in a place of saying what this relationship is because I would be taking the power away from you to make that decision, to decide for yourself. I am not going to say the relationship is this or that, but that this is the invitation.

This moment puts before you and every single human being—you decide what is the answer to Barbara's question. You decide, in fact, not just what you say, but what you think, and by your actions. Decide through the demonstration of your response, and then make it real.

Two reasons to do this, as I experience it, are:

To self-activate, so that I might know myself experientially and not just conceptually, so that I can experience what I conceive of myself.

I notice that as I move through the world in this particular way, other people's lives are touched, and they look at themselves in the mirror, and they call *me* (we are all mirrors for each other) and say, *you know what?* Exactly what Barbara just said, *I have had the same kind of experience.*

There is a lie, by the way, I should tell you. There is a lie on the cover of the first *Conversations With God* book—it is a huge lie.

The book is called *Conversations with God: An Uncommon Dialogue*. It is not an uncommon dialogue. It was the publisher who put that out there without realizing that he was telling a fib. In fact, it is a very common experience, and what is happening right now is that people are coming out of the closet. They are coming out from hiding, and they are saying you know, *I am that too*. And Barbara, Neale, Deepak, and all the others have given us permission to lay claim to our Divinity. That's the huge first step that any evolving species does and must take. I agree completely with that, and ask:

What do you think?

What are our conversations with God?

What is going on?

It's one beautiful question.

MESSIANIC CONVERSATION AND EMBRACING THE CONVERSATION WITH GOD

Marc

Neale, thank you so much for being with us.

I am thinking about the Hebrew word for *messiah*. The word *mashiach* means *siach*, conversation. That is what the word means—messiah is conversation with God. The messianic era is when people realize that that conversation is happening.

You talked about earlier how all the great religions were true but partial.

One of the visions that was true was this vision that was not realized but was there seated in potential: the democratization of enlightenment, the democratization of greatness, which is really what you are talking about.

Conversation With God stands so beautifully for that vision of the democratization of enlightenment. We started with the democratization of governance. If someone said a thousand years ago, *you are going to have a one person vote, and every person is acting to vote, power is distributed in reality,* back then, they would be burned at the stake. It was an insane thing to say. **Today, the vision of the democratization of enlightenment seems so critical because the only mechanism we have for a new politics is what Barbara and I like to call Unique Self Symphonies**. It is not just *tat tvam asi, I am that,* but I am *uniquely* that.

It is God having a Neale experience, and because God's having a Neale experience, I do not have to say, *Oh my god. Why can't I be Neale or Barbara?* I can meet Neale and say, *I am in devotion. I am delighted. I am ecstatic to meet God having a Neale experience.*

Then the Unique Self of Neale (the irreducible unique expression of that LoveIntelligence and LoveBeauty that is the initiating and animating energy of All-That-Is that lives as Neale) comes together with other Unique Selves in Unique Self Symphony. All of a sudden, the self-organizing Universe is not driven by pheromones that drive an ant colony, but by irreducible uniqueness that is Unique Self Symphony and becomes an expression of unleashing what we need to address existential risk that threatens us in a very real way.

THE HOLY TIPPING POINT: JUST ONE BLINK AWAY FROM TOTAL AWAKENING

Neale

How does the democratization of enlightenment play out?

What we are creating, Marc, is what I called in my previous writing, a civil rights movement for the soul, freeing humanity at last.

Hallelujah as we say in church. Freeing humanity at last and its belief in a violent, angry, and vindictive God. That simple shift alone, if nothing else, that movement alone could change the world overnight. Simply touch the lives of billions and billions of people (and we have the power now to do that).

By the way, we are only one click away...

As Pema Chodron[14] said, *we are one blink of an eye away from total awakening* because we do not have to awaken eight billion people, or even two billion people. Critical mass is not 51 percent. It's not 25, ten, or even five. **Critical mass, they tell us, is between two and four percent of the whole, and we are very close to that right now.**

Marc

This is the holy tipping point, and this is the *only* tipping point.

Neale, we are dedicated to a planetary awakening in love by whoever feels that love, giving that love together in a kind of symphony (such as the internet and the noosphere in Teilhard de Chardin's awakening) that is God's collective eyes. And if it takes two percent, that would be a goal of the Evolutionary Church—to help nurture that and to bring it into a certain degree of coherence.

I invite you, Neale, to be one of the greatest spokespeople. People that we can call on and quote your works and make sure that people read them in

---

14 Pema Chödrön, an American Tibetan Buddhist nun and author. In her book *Start Where You Are: A Guide to Compassionate Living*, she writes: "We already have everything we need. There is no need for self-improvement. All these trips that we lay on ourselves—the heavy-duty fearing that we're bad and hoping that we're good, the identities that we so dearly cling to, the rage, the jealousy and the addictions of all kinds—never touch our basic wealth. They are like clouds that temporarily block the sun. But all the time our warmth and brilliance are right here. This is who we really are. We are one blink of an eye away from being fully awake."

order for this to happen because we are really in an existential crisis—a breakdown which is exactly the trigger for this breakthrough.

THE POWER OF SELF-SELECTION AND MIRRORING GLOBAL CHANGE

[Neale]

I said to God, you know, this feels so big to me. I am not sure I am willing to undertake the project to save the world. God said, *whoa, whoa, whoa. Wait a minute. If you think that you need to take on the idea of saving the world, you are going to back away from that because you are going to see it as way too much.*

What we are talking about here is individual evolution.

If you simply take on the process of evolving yourself and become an example of what it means to do that, that is sufficient.

That is all that the great masters have ever done. You can do the same thing, and you are able to do that right now by simply self-selecting and saying, *you know what—that much I can do.*

I can pay enough attention to my own evolutionary process so that all those whose lives I touch wind up experiencing (by mirroring to them who they are) their own highest possibility. **The fastest way to achieve global transformation is to achieve your own transformation.**

In *Conversations with God*, God said to me, very clearly, that which you wish to produce in the lives of another, produce in your own life; and that which you wish to produce in your own life, produce in the lives of another. The two then become one.

So, I have given up the idea and am now focused highly on what I can do to move myself to the next level in my own evolutionary process.

Someone asked me: Neale, what is your last great life challenge now that you are deep into your 70s?

I answered that my last great life challenge is to walk my talk, to actually step into the experience of expressing who I declare myself to be. Let that be my final victory, my final journey, a process so that when I put my head back on the pillow for the final time, I can say, *wow, I made it. I made it.* I did it even if only for five minutes—the last five. I tell my wife all the time that if I can be there for the last five minutes of my life, I can say, *wow*.

NO ONE ELSE CAN HAVE YOUR EXPERIENCE

[Marc]

There is a new prayer that we are formulating that is based on a new credo. It is this notion that if Neale does something, there is no one else who can do that. Marc cannot do it. Barbara cannot do it. No one else in the entire world can have that experience. It's the notion of irreducible uniqueness.

Not only am I that, but I am uniquely that. So here's our credo, the answer to the question of *who are you*. The great question of *who are you*:

> You are an irreducible, unique expression of the LoveIntelligence and LoveBeauty that is the initiating and animating Eros of All-That-Is that lives in you, as you, and through you, that never was, is, or will be ever again, other than through you.

> And as such, you have an irreducibly unique perspective, taste, quality of intimacy, and presence which has the ability and capacity to give your unique gift to your unique circle of intimacy and influence.

You can stand, as Neal called the singularity of divinity, on the abyss of darkness, and say, *Let there be light.* You can speak to a corner of the world that is unloved and create love there in a way that no one who ever was, is, or will be, can do other than you.

So, you can throw away your Prozac. *Amen.*

WHEN EVERYTHING IS GREAT, THEN WHAT?

Neale

Co-creation is fantastic, but it demands individuals to do it. Isn't the idea of eternal or Divine expansion nearly the same thing as endless growth?

Let me share with you my experience of *there being no such thing as endless growth* in the human sense, and that we become larger and larger and larger.

What is increasing is our awareness that we have grown to fullness. That's what evolution is about. Evolution isn't about becoming more than what you already are. Evolution is about becoming more aware of *that* which you always were, *that* you are now, and you always will be *that*.

When we are aware of *that*, this awareness can come to us in any moment of our lives. It also, by the way, sometimes leaves us. My experience has been that I step into *that* awareness, and then sometimes I step out of it and step back into the illusion of *I am not that.*

Then I step back into awareness, and I again step out of it.

The struggle of humanity, as I experience it in my own life, is to step into that awareness and stay there.

That is the beauty of the Evolutionary Church. It allows you to find the awareness, step into the awareness, and stay right where you are. Thank you. Thank you. If the Evolutionary Church can help with that, we say glory, glory, *Hallelujah*, and we reclaim that at a higher level of consciousness, a deeper place.

In reading *Conversations with God Volume One*, you may have a dilemma: did not God voluntarily forget everything and come as us in order for us to rely only on ourselves, not needing to use His resources?

NOT CREATING, BUT REMEMBERING: THE ESSENCE OF DIVINE AWARENESS

Neale

That is a misreading and a misunderstanding of the messages of *Conversations with God* and of the ultimate universal truth.

God, of course, did not step into His/Her/Its own forgetting. Part of the process of *physicalization* is a voluntary removal of the total and complete awareness of who we are as creators.

Let me explain it: **Everything that ever was, is now, or ever will be, is now.**

The act of creation in the purest sense is impossible because everything that has been created, that ever was created, is now, and ever will be created already exists right now in the eternal moment of here and now.

If I wanted to experience myself as the creator, one who can create one's own reality and create the experience around me, I would have to do something very clever. I would act.

I would have to have what I call spiritual temporary amnesia for a split moment in time. I would have to forget that *it* (whatever I wanted to create) has already been created so that I could recreate it again by noticing the fact that *it* has always been there.

See, what we are doing? We are not really creating anything—**we are simply noticing that which we choose to experience has already been created.**

Or as somebody far more articulate once said:

> Even before you ask,
> I will have answers.
>
> Do not go around asking,
> What are we to eat?

> What are we to drink?
> Wherewithal will we clothe ourselves?
>
> Seek ye first who you really are.
>
> Seek ye first the experience of heaven and of God
> and all these things will be added unto you.
>
> —Matthew 6:33

Not because you have created them—because you have noticed that they were already created for you, and it has always been there; it's never not been there.

So, I want to say to you that God did not in fact forget anything, but we have used the clever device of temporary spiritual amnesia to allow ourselves to experience the process of creation, which is really the process of noticing that *it* always existed. *It* always is, and *it* always will be.

NEALE'S BLESSING

Neale

> We call upon the Divinity that we all are,
> that resides within each and every one of us,
> that expresses in us and through all of us.
> We call upon that essence, that pure essential essence,
> the pure energy that is us,
> to allow us to free us,
> to inform us,
> and to bless us
> with the experience of the expression
> of exactly that truth,
> in each and every moment of our lives.
> In asking and in claiming that blessing,
> we make a commitment,

a simultaneous commitment,
that our commitment is to never stop sharing that blessing
with everyone whose life we touch.
So, I bless you.
I offer you my blessing.
And I bless you at the same time that I ask you to bless me as well.
Let's bless each other.
Blessed be, that we might bless.
Amen.

MARC'S BLESSING

Marc

Neale, you speak to and invite us, to everyone, to the power of blessing, and that is *the democratization of enlightenment*. We are the priests. We are the kingdom of priests that we can give blessing, and yes, we have forgotten. But it is okay to forget. **It's only problematic when we've forgotten that we've forgotten.**

We get to remember again and to know that we are needed. To be an irreducible Unique Self is to know the great noble truth that:

Reality needs us.

Reality desires us.

Reality adores us.

Reality loves us.

Reality recognizes us.

Reality delights us.

Amen.

CHAPTER EIGHT

THE WOUND AND THE AWAKENING: TRANSFORMING PAIN INTO INTIMACY

Episode 28 — May 6, 2017

TAPPING INTO THE WOUNDING OF SEPARATION

Let's place our attention in the resonant field of the communion of visionary souls activated worldwide to express our own love and creativity into a suffering world.

Just feel us, all of us, wherever we may be throughout this church and throughout the world, seeing the world as the church in this sense. It is a global church for the sacred story of evolution. Feel the wounding of this whole world for one moment.

Think of the billions of people and how many of them are suffering from some sense of wounding. It's a planetary yearning for intimacy.

This wounding is due to an illusion of separation— among people, among nations, among religions, among professions. This illusion is intrinsic to *Homo sapiens*, **the creature that is self-conscious.**

Feel the wounding on a planetary scale, moving up to a crisis point where it is so intense that it could in many ways destroy our own environmental life-support system and our own existence. Then let's place our own personal wounding in the planetary wound.

Let's get in touch with the nature of that wound.

It is very private.

It is personal.

It is always different for different people.

Intimate wounding also comes from an experience of separation, lack of love, loss of love through separation.

How we gain power for ourselves from this wounding is, no matter how you may feel wounded, to increase intimacy.

Instead of reacting to the myriad sources of woundings and feeling excluded, hurt, rejected, or dismissed, even up to physical or health woundings, let's just take that wound, personally, silently, inside ourselves, and see if we can draw up, from within a power of increased intimacy, exactly where the wound hurts toward the person or persons that appear to be wounding us, increasing our power by increasing our intimacy. Because the truth is, no matter who this person is or how this wound developed, that person who appears to be the cause is wounded.

Your power is not just simply to forgive this person but to recognize the wounding. **Increase your intimacy toward that person no matter what or how painful, and you will feel a power of love rise in you.** We all have the ability to do that.

A memory of the greatest example we have ever had of that was the crucifixion of Jesus Christ, when he went to Jerusalem. He knew what he was facing. The disciples asked him not to go.

He said, *Get thee hence*, and I always remember this phrase, *He set his face to go to Jerusalem*. It was almost certain death by crucifixion. There cannot be a more terrible death, and here is this beautiful, sensitive man: he set his face to go to Jerusalem. When he said, on the cross, *Father, forgive them, they know not what they do*, let's, without remembering the horror of that entire experience, place this as the ultimate expression of turning wounding into power.

We can take wherever the wound is in us and say, *Father, Mother, God, forgive whoever that was,* even myself if I am the overt cause of it, *I know not what I did.* We are now rejoining with God, with power, with love, with triumph.

Then let's take the story of Jesus and reveal, after the three days in the tomb, after the crucifixion, what happened: the resurrection. The total, radical transformation of the body in person, appearing and saying, *You will do the work that I do, and greater works will you do.*

Being aware of the suffering world and seeing the illusion of separation all over the world causing that pain and being a planetary awakener through our power of love, we can do that.

This is the planetary awakening in love. This is healing, right here.

Then go to the personal pain that we may be feeling by the rejection of somebody or something that has not needed you where you needed to be needed. Send tremendous empathy to the source, that person, who themselves is suffering. We are empowered.

Let's join with the greatness of this evolutionary impulse on planet Earth, Jesus, and say, *If you have seen me, you have seen the Father.* Here I am—I am a new being. We want to take *Homo universalis* the whole way.

ENLIGHTENMENT MEANS THE WOUND IS NOT UNCONSCIOUS IN US

We have walked through both the wounding of the world and the pain that comes from lashing out when people are wounded. Of course, we have had to look at our own wounds because there is no person without wounds.

Jesus is wounded on the cross, and Jesus is wounded in whatever his early story was, and Ramana Maharshi[15] was wounded, and Gandhi was wounded. Enlightenment does not mean they are not wounded. **Enlightenment means that the wound is not unconscious in us.**

This resonance is even particularly beautiful.

There are thousands of people joining us from around the world in Evolutionary Church; we are in the new Bethlehem, and we have to set our faces to Jerusalem.

To create Evolutionary Church, we have to create a new resonance in Reality, as the world's wounds bring us to a place of potential extinction (for the first time in history). **We cannot bypass the wounds in our personal healing, and we cannot bypass the wounds in our collective healing; we enter the wounds with joy.**

We enter the wounds with a sense of knowing that most of our wounds are unconscious.

We are projecting the wound of the Father ninety-nine percent of the time.

When we are furious with someone, we see them as *my father*. We are creating instantaneous intimacy to heal the intimacy that *I did not have with my father or mother who may have died young.*

Sometimes the wounds are from our own lives.
Sometimes the wounds are intergenerational.
Sometimes they are passed on through the generations.

As we move into the prayer:

Sometimes we do a confession of greatness.
Sometimes we do a confession of vulnerability.
Sometimes we do a confession of wounding.

---

15   Ramana Maharshi (1879–1950) was a renowned Indian sage and spiritual teacher who is widely recognized for his teachings on self-inquiry and non-dualism (Advaita Vedanta). He is considered one of the most influential spiritual figures of modern India. His teachings focus on realizing the True Self as the ultimate reality and the essence of existence.

We are going to bring our wounds to the Mother in prayer—our holy and broken *Hallelujah*.

I (Marc) want to share a story, not about personal wounding but about collective wounding—the wound that we received from the previous generation.

> My mother, who I do not talk about often, was born in Stanislav, a little town in Eastern Europe. She was born into the world of the Holocaust, and she tells a story.
>
> One of my early senses of being universal and moving past a particular religion as an ethnocentric context was a Christian family that hid my mother—a beautiful, righteous Christian family that hid my mother on the pain of death during the worst years of the Holocaust.
>
> My mother is a truth teller, both in beautiful ways and sometimes in painful ways, and it is hard to argue with her truth, and bless my mother. My mother is awesome.
>
> Someone who lived next door to the family that was hiding her had come and stolen something from the family. My mother at this point was four years old. Being a four-year-old in the Holocaust was often with full grown-up faculties fully alert because survival was the game.
>
> When survival is the game, we adapt. So, my mother said to her Christian, kind of adoptive mother, *They stole this, these things from you.* Her adoptive Christian mother went and asked, *Did you guys take these things?*
>
> The neighbor said, *She's a Jew; she did it.* And they called the Gestapo to turn her in.
>
> My mother describes a Gestapo raid in which she had climbed up a tree, in which the Gestapo came in killing.

And my mother's up a tree.

And I apologize for what I am about to say, but, but we just need to note that this is part of the Reality and our tone. We need to be in radical joy and radical delight. And we live in a world of outrageous pain, and we need to be able to respond to that pain.

And as was said so beautifully, *all wounding is a failure of intimacy*. So, I need to find and make contact with the wound to heal the wound.

So, what happened was two Gestapo men, obviously tragically wounded themselves, seized a baby, and they took the baby outside, and my mother said they actually ripped the baby apart.

And I can hear my mother saying it at the table, like a wishbone. We would be at the table eating chicken on Sabbath, and my mother would see a wishbone. And she would remember that story and would tell that story time and again. It was the story of my youth. I heard the story thousands of times. That was the defining story.

At some point, when I was in my thirties, I was writing a book called *Soul Prints*. I was writing, I was kind of doing an Aurobindo[16] practice, which I still do, where I write hundreds of thousands of words, and I realized that I was the reincarnation of that baby. I actually realized, oh, that baby is me.

That is why I get ripped apart, and that I suffer. In some sense, in my life, it is part of my destiny to walk into that wound and to heal that baby. **That baby is the ultimate wound. The baby is the ultimate Eros.**

This story is the ultimate failure of Eros, the ultimate destruction. All ethical collapse comes from a failure of Eros.

---

16   Sri Aurobindo (1872–1950) was an Indian philosopher, yogi, poet, and nationalist who played a significant role in India's struggle for independence and later became a prominent spiritual leader. His teachings integrate philosophy, spirituality, and political thought, emphasizing the evolution of human consciousness and the realization of divine life on Earth.

How do we bring that baby and make that baby whole again? How do we live in a world in which a baby can be ripped apart?

If you think that is just a story from the Holocaust . . . it is happening now.

- It happened in Rwanda.
- It happened in Bosnia.
- It happened in Cambodia.
- It is happening all the time in the middle of our lives, as we are going out for dinner and doing some New Age transformative process.
- It is actually happening in the world.

In a collective world, in a global world, we take in the outrageous pain, and we respond with Outrageous Love—we walk into the wound. **Then we own the wound; we are intimate with the wound, we laugh at the wound, we *realize* the wound, and the wound opens up.** The wound opens up, and it melts.

We are all wounded, and there is a part of us that has been ripped apart.

There isn't one person that doesn't feel like they have been betrayed. We are all Jesus in some sense. Christianity is a religion built in response to being ripped apart, to having nails being driven into me. But I can only be betrayed by someone who would never betray me. That is what betrayal means. Betrayal means there is radical trust, radical love—she/he could never betray me; they could never distort my story, they could never rape my body, or rape my name. And yet it happens.

It happens because ordinary people do it to each other.

Evil does not come from monsters. Evil always comes through the wound. Evil always means we intentionally move to hurt each other because we feel wounded.

Our hymn, the holy and the broken *Hallelujah*, is about the ordinary wounds of an ordinary life.

The reason Leonard Cohen is so important, and the reason we chose him and "Hallelujah" as the hymn is because he touches the wound. See what he is doing? As Leonard says, let's look at the wound. Let's not hide the wound.

My good friend loves to read Leonard Cohen books because in his poetry, he is always touching the wound. And the reason we trust Leonard is because the wound is not disowned. It is not dispossessed, but he speaks about it as a cold victory.

Love is not a victory march. It is a cold and a broken *Hallelujah*. He talks about the wound, and because he talks about the wound, we can trust him.

When you can laugh at the wound, you are trustable.

You remember that book by Umberto Eco, *The Name of the Rose?*[17] It is about these monks who are getting poisoned when they are reading this document, and no one knows why they are being poisoned. It turns out that that document is the page of Aristotle's ethics where he talks about laughter, and some monk has poisoned that page. So, if you go and turn to that page, you get poisoned because that monk didn't want there to be laughter. It is only through laughter that we own the wound. Only through laughter can we relax into it.

As we have our wounding on the table, our intention in Evolutionary Church is to heal the source code. Our intention is to participate in the evolution of love. We are the new Jerusalem. We are the new Church.

Our goal is to create an uprising in love, an uprising in intimacy that melts the wound. An uprising in evolutionary understanding that does not bypass the wound but walks through the wound, the void, and avoids

---

17 Umberto Eco (1932–2016) was an Italian medievalist, philosopher, semiotician, novelist, cultural critic, and political and social commentator. He is best known for his 1980 novel *The Name of the Rose*, a historical mystery that combines semiotics with biblical analysis, medieval studies, and literary theory.

(a-void-dance) where we dance around the void. **We love Leonard because he never dances around the void.** Therefore, we can trust him, and we can melt the wound.

FROM EGO TO ESSENCE

I have something really wonderful to share about how to deal with a wounding.

One of my favorite teachers, A. H. Almaas,[18] had an approach to suffering that I've tried a lot and worked with a lot of people, and I'd like to read a paragraph from him and then practice together.

Almaas suggests that we directly experience the deficiency of the ego or local self and recognize what the ego is attempting to get is already present in essence—in our language what separate self is attempting to get is already present in intimacy with Source.

The process is to deeply feel ego's lack (or hole as Almaas calls it) and not defend against the feeling or come up with any strategies for solving the problem from the ego's point of view. It is a two-way process, and we'll do this first.

The Beloved (a name that I have for the deepest evolutionary self) invites the local selves to come forward to describe as deeply as possible any pain, needs, wants, or deficiency being experienced. Do not defend against the feeling. Do not try to fix or solve it. Just completely allow the feeling of the pain. Stay with that pain and follow it all the way through to the roots, the source, where we first felt the pain.

We have looked at the entire suffering of the world as an illusion of separateness in millions, hundreds of millions, and billions of forms.

---

18 A. H. Almaas, born A. Hameed Ali in 1944 in Kuwait, is an American spiritual teacher and author renowned for developing the Diamond Approach to self-realization—a methodology that integrates spiritual teachings with modern depth psychology.

> *We have seen our own illusion of our own deep suffering that comes from a loss of intimacy, a loss of love.*

Just hold it for ten seconds in this beautiful space. We are feeling the wound as deeply as we can—each of us personally. It's different for every person, but it's the same essence.

Stay with that pain and follow it all the way to the root, the source where we first felt this pain (for me, I think I first felt it when my mother died when I was about 12). It's that sense of separation, loss of love, each of us. Let's go to wherever that was that you first felt it. Sometimes it brings tears to the eyes. I feel the tears welling up in my throat even now.

According to Almaas, when we follow the deficiency, the loss of love, as deeply as possible, it leads us to that part of essence, that part of uniqueness, that is our essence which the local self has been seeking by trying some strategy in the outer world: *You better love me better. This person better love me more, or I am going to die again.*

Seeking some strategy in the outer world, we let our local selves discover that **the fulfillment it has been seeking is already present in the Beloved, in the essence, in the unique expression of divine essence.** The ego then becomes the guide to essence.

He describes it in his book called *Essence:*[19]

> When one allows oneself quietly to experience the hurtful wound and memories connected with it, the golden elixir will flow out of it, healing it, and filling the emptiness with the beautiful, sweet fullness that will melt the heart, erase the mind, and bring about the contentment that the individual has been thirsting for.

---

19 A.H. Almaas, *Essence with the Elixir of Enlightenment: The Diamond Approach to Inner Realization* (York Beach, ME: Samuel Weiser, 1998), 116.

When ego's search for satisfaction is over because you are not defending, not strategizing, it leads you to that part of the Pearl[20]—the pearl inside you, with probing intelligence; it helps the local self see that the source of the problem is its own illusion of separation.

My illusion of separation from my mother, in some sense, is very physically real. When I seek this, she is there in the Field of Resonance. The ego, the separated self, experiences a reunion with essence, with the Pearl, with the innate being. In that sense, it's never really separated from intimacy because it is Source.

The local self releases the sense or feeling of judgment on itself; it stops trying to negotiate to be right and experiences compassion for itself, taking on the vantage point of the Beloved toward itself—**the absolute essence of beingness toward itself is never separate**.

Our local selves become wise enough to see themselves through the eyes of their own Divinity. That Divinity is that essence, that pearl in each of us that's seeing the pain of separation. The pain of separation, when seen with the eyes of Divinity, does not exist. From this view, there is no right and wrong, no good and evil—only truth—and the truth sets us free of judgment. Judge not. In the resonant field, the local self is unstressed.

Let's see if we can feel that.

Egoic problems are not, in the first instance, solved. They are dissolved. Dissolved in the resonant vibrational field of the divine essence, problems fade and no longer seem to exist. As our local selves are educated, they begin to become the instruments of our own unfolding. That is what we are doing here by looking at the wound and seeing how it brings us into power.

---

20 In the teachings of A.H. Almaas, The Pearl—often referred to as "The Pearl Beyond Price"—is a metaphor for a particular stage in personal and spiritual development. It represents the integration of one's essential being (essence) with the personal self, creating a unique individuality that is both authentic and divine. The concept is extensively explored in Almaas's book, *The Pearl Beyond Price: Integration of Personality into Being, an Object Relations Approach*.

We discover that underneath all the specific symptoms which feel so personal and unique, there is usually one fundamental source from which the particular problems spring—ego's separation from essence—the feeling of being separate from the True Self, the Unique Self, and from the whole.

Yes, this is ego's separation from essence—in traditional language, the human's separation from God. Therefore:

The fundamental solution to many of our problems is the union of ego and essence on a collective scale.

The separated self joins with God and is absorbed into the godhead.

Most of our major problems are caused by social structures of top-down dominance and control, where the collective ego is in charge.

As each of us shifts our identity from ego to essence, we are making a significant contribution toward both personal and social transformation. This is a major practice of Evolutionary Church.

If I'm going to go out as a pioneer of Evolutionary Outrageous Love while my ego is really upset because *so-and-so doesn't love me*, or *my mother died when I was 12*… And if I'm going out to help everybody who is wounded, I need to be able to deal with *my* wound this way, and it is very profound.

From Almaas's book *Essence,* and from my book *Emergence: The Shift from Ego to Essence*,[21] we learn how this works, but you have to keep doing it. This doesn't work by doing it once.

We talked about the need for practice because you do not get this by just hearing about it from somebody else. This is a deep, deep practice. I would recommend it.

---

21 Barbara Marx Hubbard, *Emergence: The Shift from Ego to Essence* (Charlottesville, VA: Hampton Roads Publishing, 2001).

What our course is all about is the ultimate feeling of union and oneness with God as Source, expressing as us, leading to the tremendous empowerment of the Evolutionary Unique Self.

Unique Self is expressing joyfully like this, with all the pain, none of it denied.

That is a *whole being* right there.

Thank you everyone in this church. Let's do it together. Let's go the whole way in this lifetime.

Homo sapiens is giving birth to an emerging species that is willing to practice all this, that is not perfect, but whose yearning is great enough to carry us home.

If we can do it here, we can do it anywhere.

MY WOUND IS THE INTENTION OF THE LOVEINTELLIGENCE OF COSMOS

Unique Self teaching takes the next step in unique wounding. Many people have called Almaas and me (Marc) and said we should talk to each other and how these teachings are very deeply connected.

Here's a chant that talks about the place where I cannot quite find my place. Do not separate from me; just be with me.

What happens so often in human potential communities is that we ignore the wound, we forget about the wound, we bypass the wound, and then:

- We act out of the wound to destroy.
- We act out of the wound to smear.
- We act out of the wound to deconstruct.

Because we cannot own the wound. That's why we love Leonard Cohen—he owns the wound.

Our other hymn is about transforming the wound. Let's sing it to each other, and let's feel it with each other. This is not information but invocation—that is what this hymn is about. Let's be in this together. "How Could Anyone," Libby Roderick [*See Appendix*]

Now, watch the trajectory friends: *How could anyone ever tell you that you are less than whole* is the wound that comes from the experience of separation. I am either separate from planet Earth; I am separate from Gaia, so I am wounded, or I am separate from the Mother, so I am wounded. **But ultimately those separations mirror the deepest separation which is:** *I am separate from Source.*

What is my unique wound? How does my unique wound lead me to my Unique Self? What is this idea of separation? How do I get over this failure of intimacy that causes wounds?

When I am separate from Source:

I feel vulnerable.

I feel incomplete.

I feel fragile.

I feel alienated.

The wound always expresses separation.

In the second part of this lyric, we ask, *How could anyone fail to notice that our love is just a miracle?*

We restore intimacy. How could anyone fail to notice that? *How deeply we are connected in our souls!* We restore intimacy. It's our response to the wound. It's the restoration of intimacy.

And the Jesus story, when brought to bear, encourages us to understand that God is not only the Infinity of Power; God is the Infinity of Intimacy that loves us so much that God is also willing to be the infinity of pain, at the infinity of wounding itself.

In that great mystic, mythic story, God says, *I am willing to become man, I am willing to become woman, to participate with you in the wounding. Know that my pain is not a small pain because I am Divinity. Divinity lives in us. I am the infinity of pain.* Jesus on the cross said, *I am going to experience every pain in all pain.* Wow.

What does it mean to find each other in our tears like we find each other in our joy? What does it mean to say that no one's going to be wounded alone? What does it mean to find people who are in chronic pain, who become so lonely, so fast because no one can stay with them?

In an acute story, we stay with them. In chronic pain, we cannot stay with them.

How many lonely people... That's why people responded to the Beatles in the mid-60s when they sang, *All the lonely people... where do they all belong?*[22]

That lonely person lives in us and is the part of us that is wounded, that we put away. But here's the key: the way we want to reclaim the wounding is not that we create our identity out of the wound.

If I create my identity out of the wound, then I become a victim. And the price of becoming a victim is that I am always impotent. I am always a victim, always being wounded. I am always innocent. I am never responsible. I am never part of the story. **The price of my innocence is impotence, so I can never create my identity out of the wound.**

But, my identity is my whole self—my Unique Self. My identity is the power that comes from touching the wound and transforming it into connection, into intimate contact.

---

22   The Beatles, "Eleanor Rigby," *Revolver*, 1966.

> *The wound is the source of my aliveness.*
> *It's the source of my power.*

It's the place where I feel my inconsolable longing, my inconsolable yearning to be part of something, to connect, to be completely intimate. **It's in that wound, which reminds me and invites me to my intimacy, that I'm called forward to my greatness.**

But first, we have to confess the wound.

My deepest wound is:

> Losing my beloved son.
> My fear that, at the end of the day, I am fundamentally alone.
> Not being recognized by my father.
> That I am a bother, I am not wanted. I am not needed. I am in the way.
> I am extra.
> I am not enough.
> I do not make a difference.
> How I fear judgment.
> The abandonment of self and betrayal of love.
> I am not seen.
> Separation from my parents as a child by a long hospital stay, that still lives in me.

We confess our wounding. My deepest wound is:

> A lack of guidance in how to be in the world right, by my innocent parents.
> As a very young child, when I realized my mother was never going to be there for me.
> Remembering my separation, my mother's love, even in the womb.

I feel like I am too much, so I make myself small.
Having a stillborn daughter.
A distorted memory that I was abandoned as a toddler in the middle of the night.
We are destroying our beautiful planet.
Being gay.
Not meeting the expectations of the world.
Losing my 17-year-old son to suicide three years ago.
Holding my breath, holding my joy too timid.

By confessing our wounds and coming together, we model how it works and participate in the evolution of love. Here in Evolutionary Church, we model what it means. We model what the possibility is.

Now, let's go into joy. Let's pick up that wound and realize that that wound is the source of our aliveness. That wound wakes us up towards connection.

---

*I want to know what love is,
and I want to love it open together.*

Let's feel that Evolutionary Church is ours. Let's feel that Evolutionary Church is our gift to the world!

My deepest wound is not being seen and not belonging—it is the separation all over the world. It is so important to realize that *my* wound is the wound that *everyone* has.

When we begin to own those wounds, they get transformed, and my deep, unique wound brings me to my Unique Self because my wound is not an accident. My wound is not a mistake. My wound is the intention of the LoveIntelligence of Cosmos. My wound is the calling that invites me.

My wound is the yearning and evolution for me to be whole and give my unique gifts, so I feel the joy. I feel the joy coming on. I feel delight coming on. I feel the delight of being together coming on. I feel my joy enlivening me and calling me to my greatness.

My deepest wound is I am not loved and not welcome. How could that be? Even though I'm this talented, sophisticated, gorgeously successful human being, with kids, and a great husband, and a great practice. Yet that wound lives, just like it lives in you, me, and all of us.

> *My wound has opened me to be available and passionate to love and of life.*
> *My wound has been my passion to work with others who are unloved.*
> *My wound now brings me to co-creating a deep, loving, and sweet intimacy with my beloved self. And that sweet intimacy is needed by All-That-Is.*

I want to know what love is. I want to love it open all the way. We are in Bethlehem. We are founding an Evolutionary Church together. We do not bypass the wounds. We do not make the New Age move of thinking, "I am all light." No!

We go with Leonard Cohen: we are holy, we are a broken *Hallelujah,* and we're going to love that wound open. It's going to call us into the light. Oh my God, how gorgeous. I am going to be able to give my gift.

> *My wound helps me to see the importance of connection, letting others know that they are not alone.*
> *My wound allows me to know that my father was wounded, and when I feel my father's wound I realize it was not about me. Then I can love him and bring him back.*
> *My deepest wound has opened my heart.*
> *My wound tells me there is nothing left out.*
> *My wound leads me to take responsibility and to appreciate radically.*

My wound is the passion for creating community for extreme people, like extreme skiers that want to go all the way. Extreme skiers on the slopes of life.
My wound is taking me home.
My wounds brought me to seek connection and be a great lover of people and all beings.

We are founding the Evolutionary Church. The word *church* is too limited, but we are using it in order to up-level the consciousness around that word.

I know what Outrageous Love is, and my heart is full.

Let's feel the Reality of a world that is wounded.

CHAPTER NINE

THE KEYS TO ACTIVATING EVOLUTIONARY LOVERS

Episode 29 — May 13, 2017

OUR HEART'S DESIRE IS FOR MORE LOVE

Our focus is to heal a brokenhearted world.

Part of the existential crisis is natural in the sense that we have overgrown the womb of Earth. We have succeeded beyond our wildest dreams as a human species, and we did not know that we were ruining our environment until very, very recently.

However, there is some deeper problem than the overgrowth of the womb of Earth that causes this crisis. **The deeper problem is the illusion of separateness in the hearts of humans**. We seem to have almost a nervous system defect of the illusion of separation and the loss of empathy.

By developing all the aspects of Evolutionary Love, spiritual, personal, social, technological, all the way on up, we realize the heart's desire for all of us is for more love!

I don't care who it is; even the worst dictators, when you really get to know them, are trying for something. If you say—as somebody once said to me—*Barbara, with your view, you should interview all the dictators of the world and see what is underneath all that.*

Well yes, there is terror, fear, and anger, but underneath all of that there is a yearning for greater love.

We dedicate our work to healing the brokenhearted world, starting within ourselves. While we're facing existential crisis, and we want to liberate Evolutionary Love, and since evolution proceeds ever more by human choice than chance, what is our choice?

Ask clearly and boldly for your deepest heart's desire. Coded in that desire is the blueprint of your evolutionary potential.

Get in touch with your deepest heart's desire in the resonant field while we are facing existential crisis. Get in touch with your deepest heart's desire and recognize that this is evolution's blueprint for your fulfillment.

Realize that our deepest heart's desire is the evolutionary blueprint within each of us to evolve the world, and that as we nurture our deepest heart's desire in a Field of Evolutionary Love, we express it as our potential to evolve our world.

We can do this as the whole. Thank you, God, for this enormous evolutionary potential. This personal heart's desire. Get in touch with what is yours.

It is the fulfillment of evolution.

EVOLVING THE LINEAGES

We are evolutionary lovers. That is who we are. That is our most basic identity. We are *not* ordinary lovers. We are *evolutionary* lovers. Wow!

When we get that, we know that our deepest heart's desire is to be an evolutionary lover. Let's really understand what that means.

Barbara has been talking about Conscious Evolution. I, Marc, have been talking about Evolutionary Love, and we bring them together. Six years ago Ken Wilber and I published an essay we worked on together called *Evolutionary Love*, which is at the end of the *Unique Self* book.

When we awaken as Conscious Evolution, what that really means is, we are awakening as an evolutionary lover.

That is the deep inside of it.

I want to go backwards and forwards at the same time because it is how we can create this church. Why are we calling it a *church*? Because we want to draw from:

- The synagogue
- The mosque
- The church
- The ashram
- Fom all the lineages

I (Marc) am, right now, in an ashram. At this very second, I am visiting one of the great men in the world, who is the successor of Rudrananda, a great teacher that died in 1973 in a plane crash into the side of a mountain. Rudrananda brought Muktananda and worked closely with Werner Erhard. Muktananda's successor was a man named Swami Chetanananda who started the *ReVision* journal with Ken Wilber, our good friend.

I am in Swami Chetanananda's ashram. It's called *The Movement Center* in Portland, Oregon. I am looking here at Abhinavagupta's *Tantraloka* in book 29. There is a lecture series given here by a man named Alexis Sanderson who was the greatest professor of Sanskrit in the world, from Oxford, who now lives here. That is the lineage.

But we can't just go back to the lineage. You have to go back to the lineage and then bring it forward. **Evolution then picks up all of the old lineages and evolution itself becomes part of the lineage.**

We can't just go backwards. We have to go backwards, take the deepest impulse and then pulsate that forward. Abhinavagupta was a major philosopher and spiritual master of the lineage of Kashmir Shaivism which is the lineage of this ashram where I am right now.

Kashmir Shaivism is all about the pulsation of the Divine in the Cosmos.

But now we realize—in a way that Abhinavagupta never could have—that *pulsation* is evolving. That I am not just going back and accessing that pulsation. **That pulsation is evolving in me, and that love that Abhinavagupta felt is Evolutionary Love.**

It is reaching forward. Wanting more. And my desire for more is that evolutionary impulse awakening in me.

WE LIVE IN A WORLD OF BROKEN HEARTS

I share with you an image that comes from the *Kabbalists*, which is my (Marc's) lineage, the lineage that I live in—even while I am a world spirituality and an evolutionary new vision person. I have a source lineage in me which is Kabbalah.

Barbara's lineage is the New Testament, and she has evolved it as the beautiful evolutionary New Testament. The lineage of the Hebrew mystics lives in me. For the Hebrew mystics, when the divine force emanates light into the world, the light enters vessels. The vessels receive the thrusting light and hold the light.

But the light is too intense because the vessels are not connected to each other. Each vessel is saying, *ana emloch—I will rule!*—my network, my mailing list—*I will rule*. So the vessels shatter. It's called *shevirat hakeilim*—the shattering of the vessels.

We live in a world of broken hearts and broken vessels.

It's *only* when we enter into our broken heart and find in the place of the broken heart, that the hidden light is found.

My lineage master, Mordechai Lainer, who died 150 years ago, spoke it into my heart, his transmission. He said, *The master...* (and, we are *all* masters. We are democratizing enlightenment. We *are* the enlightened ones. We are the ones we have been waiting for. It is *our* turn.)

He said, *The master enters into the broken vessel and liberates the spark of light in the broken vessel.*

The broken vessel is no more and no less than our broken hearts, dearest beloveds.

All of us together.

It is not you, it is all of us, we are it.

We are founding the church of broken hearts knowing that *there's nothing more whole than a broken heart*.

It is *only* if we liberate the spark in our broken heart that we can open up and be a vessel for Evolutionary Love.

The two mistakes are if we bypass the brokenness of our heart, or if we get stuck in it. We bypass it. We cover it up. We ignore it. We get stuck in it. We are stuck in our wound. We make our wound our story and our identity—instead of knowing that those wounds are the wounds of love, inflicted by the intention of *samsara* in order to be transformed into *nirvana*.

It is only then that we become evolutionary lovers.

We are imperfect vessels for the light. We refuse to bypass the broken heart. Find your deepest desire, from *within the broken heart*, and do the work of transforming the wound and *unclenching* because there is only one thing we can do in every moment of our lives: We are either opening or closing.

We always *think* that we can overcome the *clench* and open our hearts in some *theoretical* way.

But it is always like, *wow, I don't like something*, so I am clenched. We are imperfect vessels for the light. **We are *all* imperfect vessels for the light.**

We are going to go in as those imperfect vessels for the light that we are.

But it has been said, in a line from the poem "Andrea del Sarto," by Robert Browning, *A man's reach should exceed his grasp, or what's a heaven for?* Let's reach all the way. Let's bring it down now.

We offer our prayer to:

- The Divinity that is us but that's also beyond us. She holds us.
- The Infinity of Intimacy that holds the holy and the broken *Hallelujah*.

Ramakrishna would go before the altar and scream, *Mother*! He wasn't an idol worshiper. He wasn't lost in a fundamentalist Divinity.

He *felt* the Infinity of Intimacy that knows our name and holds our uniqueness, who knows exactly how we feel when we wake up in the morning. **Ramakrishna knew that we are never alone and that wherever we fall, we fall into Her hands.**

Wow!

We offer up our deepest prayer, our deepest heart's desire for ourselves and for the world.

We don't skip ourselves.

It is only by going *into* our broken heart and offering our heart's desire that we create the world of Evolutionary Love.

We are going to go through the Five Keys of creating that world of Evolutionary Love that we are waiting for—*a world in which Outrageous Love becomes the currency of connection for all human beings.*

THE FIRST KEY: THE ACTIVATION OF THE NEW IDENTITY

The context of the Five Keys is everybody's unique heart's desire encoded in the Unique Self Symphony, symphonizing towards the purpose of life on this Earth, which is the Planetary Awakening in Love.

In order to really get the importance of that—which is the context in which we are activating the Five Keys, here is this paragraph:

Humanity is working for the planetary awakening in love. Your unique heart's desire is the evolutionary purpose in every one of us.

Right there. We want to give thanks to God. Isn't this a great plan? That your deepest heart's desire is your evolutionary purpose, which has to be the purpose of evolution itself, in you. This is an awakening of a massive awareness.

What are the keys to accelerate this in each one of us? The first of the keys is: Identity.

What is my identity in this context?

My identity is one who identifies with the impulse of evolution within me that is yearning and desiring for more life, more love, and more creativity.

In our evolutionary identity, we are saying, *Yes*! The *Yes* is within the context of the planetary awakening. What your *Yes* means here is the *Yes* to *the God-Force as you.*

Your evolutionary heart's desire is the way God expresses through you, and as you, to create you.

Yes!

Go beyond the existential crisis of birth. Let's call it an existential crisis of birth of the new humanity. Let's just get over it having been a great mistake. Birth is not a mistake, but it is extremely dangerous.

We do know that the existential crisis is for the birth of a humanity that heals our broken heart through expressing our identity as love and to accelerate that in a way of doing it together.

I can tell you, from many years of practice, I learned a lot by trying. I learned a lot by practicing. Get in touch with your identity as your deepest heart's desire, as your way of healing the brokenheartedness of the world by fulfilling the deep-heartedness in yourself!

We are lifting depression and anxiety by activating a new identity. The *Yes* is the whole thing. We are in! So, what is the context?

Again, the context is a planetary awakening in love through Unique Self Symphony.

That is the greatest vision. We stake our lives on this. That vision is not a New Age vision; it is not metaphoric. As we get to the fifth key, when we talk about Unique Self Symphony, we are going to talk about how that happens. But our first key is the activation of a new identity.

What emerges out of the new identity is: *Yes!* What is the new identity? The realization that we are an irreducibly unique expression of Evolutionary Love that never was, is, or will be ever again.

We begin to understand that depression happens, that anxiety happens because of a breakdown of identity. We live in the age of anxiety. There is more anxiety, more depression and more "Prozacian" angst than in any other generation in history. We've never had this level of dislocation, mental illness, ever, because there is a breakdown in identity.

There was a premodern identity which was the great religions: I am Jewish, I am Buddhist, I am Christian. That is my identity. I know my role, okay?

Then along came modernity and that exploded that identity in many, many ways. Then there was a modern identity: I have to be successful. I have to achieve. I have to get a high school education. I have to do…modern identity.

Then along came postmodernity and it exploded modern identity, but postmodernity forgot to do something: it did not give us a new vision of identity. All of a sudden, we have lost our source of self—think Charles Taylor, the greatest book ever, *Sources of Self*. **All of a sudden, self is not sourced, and we need a new vision of identity.** Remember *The Stranger* by Camus? It was about Meursault's mother dying.

He says, *My mother died today. Or was it yesterday?*

Meaning: identity—the basic identity in the relationships of our lives—doesn't matter anymore.

In this first new key, *Who am I?*

I am a Unique Self!

I am an Evolutionary Unique Self!

I matter infinitely.

Evolution is literally awakening in me.

That is my identity. It is not a metaphor. It is not an adage. It is not a psychological trick.

It is sanity to know we are evolution having a unique experience.

And if we don't give our unique gift, be our unique presence, and be the unique quality of intimacy that is us—then evolution is stalled.

When we activate that identity, the first level of depression lifts. The first level of anxiety lifts. That new identity is rooted in the second key.

THE SECOND KEY: MY NEW IDENTITY IS ROOTED IN A NEW WORLDVIEW

This is the transition:

Premodernity had a worldview.

Buddhism had its worldview.

Christianity had its worldview,

Judaism had its worldview.

But they were all related. It was basically obedience. There was a deep inner sense of Reality, and the human being was somehow obedient, somehow aligning with eternity. That was the worldview, but we did not understand science.

- We did not understand the scientific method.
- We did not understand psychology.
- We did not understand evolution.

Modernity came and exploded the premodern worldview. Instead it was about progress, done by separate selves, in a mechanistic, scientific world. We are going to have science heal the world.

Then we blew it up.

What do we need? We need a new worldview, and that new worldview is, The Universe: A Love Story, going to ever higher consciousness, greater freedom, and more loving order. The Universe context makes this all exactly inevitable—if we say yes to it—since we have freedom in the system.

> *The new identity is rooted in The Universe: A Love Story, from the attraction of quarks, electrons, protons and neutrons in allurement to each other.*

We let that allurement towards each other join into creativity of an evolutionary order of love, then I realize that the brokenhearted world is by the broken hearts of all of us in it, feeling separate and killing each other and the environment.

You see, it may sound abstract: The Universe: A Love Story—*we are going to higher consciousness, freedom, and order*. But, if you put yourself in there, with your deepest heart's desire for the expression of *your* creative potential and God *in you* expressing—this is the direction of the Universe.

God is on our side.

My (Marc's) kids used to say, *The Force is with us*. The Force *is* with us. That's why they had *Star Wars*. We have to have the next level after *Star Wars*. We are evolutionary evangelicals

We have to have the second level after *Star Wars*, and this is activating the second key: **Find that part in you.**

We think the evangelicals are excited, and since their excitement is premodern—it is often homophobic and often anti-feminist, so we dismiss their excitement. We dismiss *enthusiasm*. We dismiss being evangelical. In truth, we are evolutionary evangelicals because evangelism means bringing the good news.

The good news is that the world does not need to teeter on the brink of existential risk and then into massive suffering.

Let's really understand. What is arousing this excitement is the knowing of who I am, which is the first key.

Imagine the excitement: you have a call from the Prime Minister, or the President, who said, *Oh my god! I need you. Your unique, gorgeous quality of intimacy and gift is utterly needed in the world,* and they knew everything about you. Would you not get off that call ecstatic? Of course you would!

We are evangelicals. We are evolutionary evangelicals.

To review:

- The first key is activating your new identity.
- The second key is that my new identity is rooted in this new worldview.

This worldview is—just like the Renaissance offered a new vision, a transformation of identity—rooted in a new vision of the world.

Michelangelo's *David* and the Medicis in Florence, changed the worldview. We are committed to this project of gathering the new Medicis. We are going to gather the new Medicis. We are going to gather the new Medicis and invest in the world, deploy in the world, this new worldview.

This evolutionary worldview is not evolution as a theory *out there* but the realization that the evolutionary impulse is moving forward and the *Universe is a love story.*

It is a love story!

That is not a metaphor.

That is not a New Age idea.

That is not a Harlequin romance.

It is the agony and the ecstasy. **It is allurement, *all the way up* and *all the way down*.** We stake our lives together to download into Reality its deepest truth: The Universe: A Love Story.

To review and said slightly differently:

- **The first key:** I am a unique expression of Evolutionary Love.
- **The second key:** the Universe, the basic memetic structure of Reality, is a love story.

Until our friends Sergei Brin and Larry Page get this, Google's not going to work, and the algorithms aren't going to work because what it means is that our personal love story is a chapter and verse in The Universe: a Love Story.

All of a sudden life begins to make sense.

We go to the third key. We begin to do evolutionary practice and create evolutionary rituals that makes this alive in us and alive in the world, because that is how we transform Reality.

THE THIRD KEY: ACTIVATING EVOLUTIONARY PRACTICE IN A PROFOUND AND DEEP WAY

I, Barbara, have been an inventor of evolutionary practice. I can see that now because I did feel this impulse in me, yearning, to address itself. I had nowhere to go to say *Yes* to that impulse because nobody could understand exactly what I was feeling at all.

I tried to belong to ordinary churches. I tried to become an Episcopalian. I really did try! I asked the minister at the church, *Tell me, is any of this true?* And the minister said to me, *Young lady, go to Sunday school.*

I went to Sunday school. The first thing I heard was, *the problem was Eve.* She seemed to want to know God, directly. That was the whole problem! I thought, *Oh my god, I am Eve incarnate here.* I left the church, and I began to search. Here's what I found:

The practice is connecting with the evolutionary impulse in me yearning to create, to love, to be.

I would say the essence of all my practices—in journal writing, in small group work, in working with the shift from my ego to my essence, in working with identifying this evolutionary impulse and saying *Yes* to it—has been activating the evolutionary impulse of love inside myself as a co-creator, uniquely, of *it*.

That led me to practice it by communicating it. It seems like we have a new pattern here, where more and more of it is coming together. Here's the thing, the evolutionary practices that I have done have led to me saying *Yes*. And that also led me to saying *Yes* to participating together in creating more of this, because I couldn't do it alone.

Something essential about evolutionary practice is you have to find those you can co-create with; this is not something you do all alone.

One of the keys of the communion groups, in practice, is sharing the heart's desire. It is a wonderful practice, to do it intimately.

To cultivate it and then *place your heart's desire in the story of creation* so you don't feel like your heart's desire is a separate thing just for you to try to do. You see it with the impulse of the irresistible force of creation.

It is then, when you've said yes to the evolutionary impulse, that it starts leading you forward into initiating action in the world.

You have to initiate your action in different areas of the world to try it out. Every action is dealing with something to do with the existential crisis, either overcoming it or activating love. When you do those practices you become an activator in the world with others who need to receive what you need to give, in order for them to give what they need to give.

THE FOURTH KEY: WHEEL OF CO-CREATION 2.0

The fourth key is a new map we are calling the *Wheel of Co-Creation 2.0*.

It brings together all of Barbara's work for decades and my (Marc's) work for decades.

(When I say Barbara's work I mean Barbara and dozens of other people that she's worked with and was inspired by. When I say *my* work, I don't mean Marc's, I mean dozens of other people that I've worked with and been inspired by. They're all with us; no one is alone.)

This *Wheel of Co-Creation 2.0* is a new navigating system created by us. It is the activation of the new map, a compass, and a symbol.

Barbara's beautiful and crucial notion of connecting co-creators worldwide, who are the leading edge of each of the twelve sectors of the wheel, is Wheel 1.0.

We added a second wheel inset to the first, which has twelve sectors expressing twelve dimensions of Unique Self expression—through which the Unique Self living his or her irreducibly unique expression of LoveIntelligence and **giving his or her unique gift affects the entire Field of Reality.**

This is the Wheel 2.0.

You start moving from role mate to soul mate to whole mate in that wheel—to feel, to cultivate, to find your partners to create with.

THE FIFTH KEY: ACTIVATING AN EVOLUTIONARY COMMUNITY

We can be part of ten communities, and they are beautiful and holy, and deep bow to all of our communities. But that's not going to activate Evolutionary Love.

> *Evolutionary community is that sensual longing to be with people who are yearning to play a larger game and to participate in the evolution of love.*

We are going to be activated together: A small group of people who can work closely together to become and model the fifth key, which is to become together a Unique Self Symphony.

We are really inviting you. Step up. Find a way in and be with us.

CHAPTER TEN

THE GLORY OF THE WOUND: TRANSFORMING PAIN INTO PURPOSE

Episode 30 — May 20, 2017

MY EYES HAVE SEEN THE GLORY OF THE WOUND

Take a moment to get in touch with the depth of your personal wound, the deepest part of it, unique to everyone.

Take that wound and place it in the planetary wound of our culture, of our entire planetary body. Just as our great unique creativity is part of the planetary awakening, so too our deepest wound is part of the planetary birthing of new humanity.

Let's place our individual wounds in the existential crisis on planet Earth. This is more than a problem. This is more than climate change. This is more than even the thermonuclear bombs. This is a complexity of crises that cannot be resolved by doing more of the same. **It is the first time in the history of this planet that any species has recognized an existential crisis that we ourselves are participating in creating.**

Place your wound in the planetary wound of our culture and ask: What is its greatest life-oriented expression that heals the wound and releases humanity from its existential crisis through your participation in it?

Get in touch with the wound as a signal and direction of expression of radically new creativity in you. Just as a crisis of birth is radically painful and produces a new child, so too our existential wounding is activating (in each of us) the unique expression that would, without the crisis, otherwise never come out.

We ask each other, deep down, what is our response to the existential crisis of wounding with that part of the pain that is guiding us to give our greatest gift?

WE ARE NOT WOUNDED BY ACCIDENT

We are here this week together in joy, in delight. **We are here to experience, and it is such a paradoxical phrase, the delight of walking through the wound, the delight of accessing the deepest place of wound, and knowing that that wound is ultimately going to be the map to our joy— the map to our transformation.**

We are here to know that we are not wounded by accident. The journey of our lives is to experience the pain of the wound, which no one escapes, and to transform that wound into a glory beyond imagination.

There is a famous story in the Ming dynasty of a plate that had been scratched that the emperor invited all of the great artisans to repair. It was a terrible scratch on this priceless bowl, which was the great expression and incarnation of art in the Ming Dynasty.

No one was able to do it, until one artisan came along and redesigned the essential artistic presentation in a way that the scratch, the blemish, became central to the design, and a beauty became available that was more resplendent, more stunning than was ever possible before.

Paradoxically, the gorgeousness of life is my unique wound because everybody is wounded, uniquely. It is not the source of my downfall; it is not the origin of my breakdown. It is actually the energy, motivation, and delight that causes my breakthrough.

The only way you can break through is to stop avoiding. We stop avoidance—a-void-dance is all the ways we dance around the void.

And we enter into our very particular wound. We do not try to paper it over. We do not try to cover it up, but we look at it fearlessly and without shame.

It is without shame because that is how we are constructed. We are designed to have a flaw in our design. Isn't that wild to realize?

WE ARE DESIGNED TO HAVE A FLAW IN OUR DESIGN

There is no one without a flaw in their design, not one person.

Alice Miller[23], my good friend, wrote a book, *Prisoners of Childhood*[24], that was later retitled, *Drama of the Gifted Child*, because, of course, who wants to buy a book called *Prisoners of Childhood*? But we would buy a book called *Drama of the Gifted Child* because *it is about me! I am the gifted child.* Works better, right? It became a major bestseller.

Alice Miller talks about her major idea (which is wrong) that we are destroyed by the tragedy of childhood. She literally calls us *survivors* of

---

23 Alice Miller (1923–2010) was a renowned Swiss psychologist and psychoanalyst best known for her pioneering work on the effects of childhood trauma on the development of the individual. Her work was instrumental in drawing attention to the ways in which abusive or neglectful childhood experiences can shape adult behavior, emotions, and mental health.

24 Alice Miller, *Das Drama des begabten Kindes: Und die Suche nach dem wahren Selbst* (Frankfurt am Main: Suhrkamp Verlag, 1979). Alice Miller, *The Drama of the Gifted Child*, trans. Ruth Ward (New York: Basic Books, 1981).

our own personal holocaust. That is the kind of terminology she uses, and that is the great horror of life, which we spend our lives barely recovering from. (Well, that's not quite true.) She says that it is essential to the nature of childhood. (Not quite true.) We are not destroyed by childhood.

Childhood is an imperfect place, and it is designed as such.

- No matter how good our parents are
- No matter how attuned they are to us
- No matter how good they are at soothing us
- No matter how good they are at delighting us
- No matter how good they are at comforting us
- No matter how good our parents are

While these are critical needs for a well-adjusted, healthy-attachment child, we are still going to feel *not received* in some way. We are still going to feel systematically misrecognized because there is a misfit in life itself.

LIFE IS DESIGNED TO BE A MISFIT

It is only in healing that, in transforming that, in recovering that, intentionally, that we come alive. We break through.

Plato wrote,[25] *All knowledge is recovery*. We know, we forget, we recover. That's in the perennial philosophy. When we gather everything from all the great thinkers, meditators, and realizers in the world, they have something called the perennial philosophy, which tells us there are seven pieces to it. I will not give you all of them, but one is:

You always get wounded, and it is in the recovery from the wound that transformation happens. Everybody experiences a holy and a broken *Hallelujah*. There is no one who does not. And that is why we love our psalm because you cannot bypass the broken *Hallelujah*. It is only by going

---

25 Plato, *Phaedo*, trans. G.M.A. Grube (Indianapolis: Hackett Publishing Company, 1997), 73a.

into the broken *Hallelujah* that we realize that the word *shever*, broken, also means nourishment.

Remember Joseph and his amazing technicolor dreamcoat? We love scriptures: Hindu, Christian, Jewish, Buddhist, scientific… all the scriptures.

And we have scripture on this:

Joseph saw there was nourishment in Egypt. Joseph saw there was *breaking, wounding,* in Egypt. **The word for nourishment, which sustains you and saves you in the time of famine, is the same word for breaking.**

Our nourishment and our transformation is by walking into and identifying our unique shadow, our unique wound, and turning that into the very lever, the very Archimedes lever, the fulcrum, by which we can change our lives.

From this place we offer our prayer.

We invite everyone; Reality invites everyone to up-level, and bring our wounds before the Mother, just as Ramakrishna[26] would cry out in his temple, *Mother, Mother, Mother.*

Prayer affirms the dignity of personal need. Prayer is heard by the Infinity of Intimacy. No word is extra.

We reclaim prayer. Not just *I am God*, but *God holds me*. The Infinity of Intimacy knows me and holds me, so I offer my prayer.

---

26 Ramakrishna (1836–1886) was a highly influential Indian mystic and spiritual teacher whose life and teachings played a pivotal role in the revival of Hindu spirituality in the nineteenth century. His real name was Gadadhar Chattopadhyay, and he is best known for his deep devotion, spiritual practices, and inclusiveness of different religious paths. Ramakrishna is widely known for his intense devotion to the Divine Mother, particularly in the form of Kali, and for his heartfelt prayers and emotional cries of "Mother, Mother, Mother!"

THE GLORY OF THE WOUND

The gates of prayer are never closed. When I pray, I am impressing my lips onto the personal face of Cosmos that hears my prayer, and Cosmos is moved. There's not one prayer that's ever unanswered. The answer is not always the *Yes* that we think it should be or the way we think it should be, but every prayer is heard, and prayers shift Reality.

Larry Dossey[27] did an incredible book gathering all the double-blind studies on the effect of prayer that we now feel and scientifically realize in the world.

Hallelujah. The gates are open, and we pray together, and we reclaim God.

Not God as the fundamentalist God, but God as the source of all creativity, God who knows me and holds me. We fall into the arms of the Beloved.

We reclaim prayer.

We loosen the fundamentalist grip on prayer to a homophobic, ethnocentric god, in which we are purely obedient, subject, and submissive. **We claim prayer as the full dignity of our mad love with the Divine and the Divine's mad love of us**—the Infinity of Intimacy holding us and knowing our name.

Let prayer spread to the world, together with activism, where we become and are the Divine. We can only get there on the route and the path that enters into the wound and transforms the wound into full joy.

---

27 Larry Dossey, M.D., is a prominent American physician, author, and advocate for the integration of spirituality and healing in modern medicine. He is best known for his work in exploring the relationship between prayer, consciousness, and health. His books and research have had a significant impact on the fields of mind-body medicine and integrative healthcare.

A CALL FOR WOUNDING TO RISE UP IN CREATIVITY

We are experiencing something so powerful as we allow ourselves to consider the existential crisis, which is different than all of our personal crises put together.

The existential crisis is a crisis in evolution itself. If we step back and look at the spiral of evolution, we will see existential crisis after existential crisis—which means that nature is telling us we cannot go on or survive as before. Most species went extinct during an existential crisis.

In an Evolutionary Church heralding Evolutionary Love as a response to both personal crises and social crises, existential crisis is a crisis of the birth of a new species. **In the past, existential crises created radical newness.**

Take a penetrating view of the existential crisis in terms of what you consider to be the most pertinent wound of your being. It's the part of you that somehow did not get fully expressed in such a way that you could give your gift, and that is still holding in you.

Let's look at the birth crisis of this new humanity as a call for that wounding to rise up in creativity.

We are calling the woman, the feminine co-creator. You remember when Jesus said, *If you have seen me, you have seen the father.*[28] This is in the most terrible type of crisis that he was facing.

What we say using the feminine form as a feminine co-creator, *If you have seen me, you have seen the Mother, Father, God.*

How is the feminine co-creator in you and me responding to the personal wound inside that has been projected onto the wound of the world? This wound is ready to destroy this form of existence. Let's hold that for a moment to see if something rises up in you.

---

28 John 14:9.

Is it possible that your greatest wound is your greatest gift? It is different than a prayer. It is a complete and total recognition and affirmation. Ask yourself this question.

The masculine co-creators have carried the wound of the masculine world—wounded and wounding—because you were called to wound in order to preserve life, to fight, to kill; we recently killed hundreds of millions of people. Wow. Think of the ones who flew those planes that dropped the atomic bomb. I (Barbara) happen to know the man who did it, and he was very proud.

In the existential crisis now, we are healing the wounds of the masculine co-creator personally, and we allow healing to expand to everyone in the world—masculine and feminine. We are co-creators calling for everyone's greatness to be expressed.

Let's add an evolutionary thought here that makes this amazingly powerful.

Nature, for billions of years, takes jumps through connecting separate innovations together to make a new whole.

Think of your existential wound healing a crisis. That is not a mistake; it is a birth of a new species, a new human, a new Earth, new worlds on Earth, new worlds in space, new worlds in the human mind.

Place your deepest impulse into that, as a feminine co-creator and as a masculine co-creator. Then let's make a gesture of synergy among everything that is emergent now, right now. Wave a magic wand and create a vehicle through which everything that's rising will be attracted in the evolution of intimacy to increase the intimacy among co-creators joining genius, as we like to say.

What is the form in which we are going to be doing this? It is a wheel we are reinventing. We call it the Wheel of Co-Creation 2.0. Why the wheel? Because everything is included in the wheel.

We have the wrong structure in society, which is that everything is separated. Cultures are separated. Disciplines are separated. People are separated by age, category, and color.

We are over that now.

The Church of Evolutionary Love is in the wheel at this moment of existential crisis, and each of us in this church is giving forth uniqueness. When we say *giving forth uniqueness*, we're placing the word *uniqueness* and the word *Essential Self* into the impulse of creation—embodied, incarnate—as each of us in a wheel of synergy.

We are connecting what is coming through us with the great pioneers of evolutionary innovation in health, education, economics, science, and technology who are now on planet Earth.

The great innovators of our time are joining us in this wheel at this moment, and we, as members of a Unique Self Symphony, are helping the great innovators synergize instead of competing.

We are calling upon the broken *Hallelujah* to warm our hearts and heal our wounds.

As in the early church there was an expectation of the Second Coming of Christ that held people through the most awesome difficulties, let's take our awareness of the planetary awakening in love through a Unique Self Symphony as our goal.

The Second Coming of Christ, the return of all the great avatars of our species, is implicit in the planetary awakening in love. So, let's call them all in from all quadrants of the Earth, all the various evolutionary inspirers of humanity. We are saying *thank you, now it is our turn*.

Such *glory Hallelujah* it is for it to be our turn in the Wheel of Co-Creation at this time of planetary existential crisis, awakening uniqueness in love, in synergy with the great geniuses of our planet, called together right now to be with all of us.

OUR WOUND CHANGES BASED ON WHO WE EXPERIENCE OURSELVES TO BE

We are talking about wounds this week, friends, and we are about to go into a practice; we are going to do our confession of greatness. Let's just feel this deeply, my friends.

What does that have to do with wounds? What does the Wheel of Co-Creation have to do with the wounds and what we call Wheel 2.0? What does it mean?

The Wheel of Co-Creation, Wheel 2.0, is when co-creators are connected worldwide at the leading edge of innovation. That's one turn of the wheel.

In a second turn of the wheel, we have this experience of Unique Self Symphony, in which we experience and know that each one of us has the actual pleasure of affecting the whole story. Then in the world of systems theory, chaos theory, and complexity theory, we realize that everything's completely interconnected. **Since everything's connected, then the gift we give actually affects and evolves the whole in a way that is palpable and real.**

But what does it have to do with wounds? Well, the answer is it has everything to do with it. The way we approach our wound changes based on who we experience ourselves to be—that is the essence and the core of the whole thing.

If I am simply a separate self, I am a skin-encapsulated ego, and then even though I have some general relationships to other people, I am a consumer. I consume goods and services, and I live as a citizen in a democracy. But basically, I am a separate self. My rights come from me being a separate self, and ultimately, I have no essential relationship to anything else.

The entire story of my life is the story of me. That is my whole story, and in the story of me, my wounds play a very, very large part because that is the unique drama of my life.

And since my life needs Eros, aliveness, and drama, I find the drama through the trauma. The drama comes through the trauma, and since I need drama, I need significance. When I need to feel like my life is enlivened, I find the aliveness through the pain; I find it through the drama and trauma of my life, the trauma coming through the drama because that is the story that I have.

What if I am inextricably part of, not separate from, the larger Field of Existence, as is self-evident today in science?

What if I know the realization of the interior sciences, and I realize that I am completely connected and intimate with all those people who surround me, and that we are part of a larger Field of Consciousness that is one field in one heart and one Reality?

I know that I am not separate. I am unique (those are completely different). I am part of the seamless coat of the Universe, but then I realize that the coat is seamless, not featureless. My unique feature is the individuated expression of the mind-heart of God living as me, in service, devotion, and delight.

- I am called to my service.
- I am called to the delight of my devotion.
- I am called to the delight of my reaching my hand out.

EXTEND YOUR HAND AND FEEL THE ONE WOUND, THE ONE LOVE

When I reach my hand out, I realize it is one wound, one love, and one heart. I shatter my narcissism with the extension of my hand.

When I extend my hand, something happens. We have scripture on this.

In the first testament, in the book of Genesis,[29] Hagar is in the desert, and she is consumed by her wound because Abraham has wounded her. Her

---

29 Genesis, Chapter 21.

husband has offended her. And her son, Ishmael, is broken through this wounding.

She places him far away so as not to see the destruction of his death. She's devastated. And then a voice of conscience, a voice of the Divine, reaches out to her and says, *Lift your hand, stretch your hand towards the boy and lift him up.*

And in that outstretching of her hand, and in that lifting up of the boy, the one who needs her, who needs her service, the circle of her narcissism is shattered, and her heart opens in devotion and in service.

The only way to shatter the oppression of the wound is to realize it is not all about me. I honor the wound. I offer the wound up to the Mother. I do my psychological work with the wound, but that is not my identity.

My identity is not my wound. My identity is my delight, my service, my joy.

My devotion, my identity, is my unique quality of presence and intimacy that never was, is, or will be. My identity is the unique expression of LoveIntelligence and LoveBeauty intended by All-That-Is that flows through me.

My identity is the unique gift that I have to give to my unique circle of influence and intimacy that can be given only by me in this moment of existential risk, in this moment when we have moved past the first shock of existence (which is the realization that I die).

We are now encountering the second shock of existence, which means that after all of the human innovations, we are now facing the possible death, not of the individual, but the death of the planet.

I begin to realize that I have something to say or do in response to that. My unique innovation is in the ways:

- I raise my children.
- I speak to the grocer.
- I work my wounds.
- I offer service in my community.
- I access the new evolutionary story.

My voice can be spoken into the noosphere, and I can know that by taking my unique stand, as systems theory and complexity theory remind us, it matters to All-That-Is.

Taking my unique stand in my personal transformation, offering my service, and offering my devotion changes everything.

Then I realize I have to confess my greatness, not just my wounds; that my wound gets transformed into my greatness; my wound shows me the way to my greatness; my wound is part of the intention of Cosmos, which is a world in which the vessels are shattered.

In the original mystical vision of the *Kabbalah*, the vessels shattered, and I am in the night of light, so I go into the shattered vessel, and I liberate the spark of light in the vessel. I do that through walking through my brokenness and transforming my brokenness.

The only way I can find my way into the broken vessel is through my own broken heart.

It's then I realize, oh my God, there is nothing more whole than a broken heart, and that every breakdown leads to breakthrough.

Then my wound is the intention of the Christ kissing me, and the intention of Krishna dancing with Radha, and the intention of Rama and Sita, and the intention of Buddha, and the intention of the great Earth and sky, and the never-ending sky, under which Kublai Khan established his kingdom. It is all one, it is all the same.

THE GLORY OF THE WOUND

We are going to bring our unguarded hearts, and we are going to confess our wound *and* our greatness.

This is a hard one, but let's see if we can get the practice: *We confess our wound, and right next to it, we confess our greatness. Just look at them together, and you'll begin to see the connection.*

Here is a model for confessions of wound and greatness:

> So, I (Marc) confess my wound.
> I confess my wound, which is the brokenness of the Holocaust that I received in my family.
> That is my wound.
> Then, I confess my greatness.
> My utter commitment is to stand on the side of light against darkness.

We confess our wound. Nothing is more whole than our broken hearts.

And to everyone, confess your wound and confess your greatness.

Here are some confessions of wounds and greatness:

- I confess my wound of not feeling a part of. I have a gift for seeing, knowing, I confess my greatness: Unity, consciousness, unconditional life for all love.
- I confess my wound of arrogance. I confess that my greatness is the audacity to believe that I can make a unique contribution to the healing of the world's suffering.
- I feel lonely; that is my wound. My greatness is that I can stay with wounded people, and I come alive through feeling life.
- I confess that my wound is not feeling seen and heard. My greatness is selflessness and dedication to my family. In my invisibility, I find my devotion. Then in my devotion, I am seen.
- I confess my wound of feeling unworthy. I confess my

greatness to be an erotic, Outrageous Lover.
- I confess the brokenness of my abuse, my being sexually abused. I confess my greatness as standing in the holy goodness and gorgeousness of teaching the sacredness of sexuality.
- I might say I confess my wound of being a child of privilege. So therefore, I have to be narcissistic. I couldn't feel the pain of others, and then I confess my greatness so that I shatter my narcissism and stand in integrity as a deep lover of Reality and the people closest to me.
- I confess my wound of not being believed; my greatness is in believing the vision.
- I confess my wound, which is a state of self-obsession. I confess my greatness, which is a state of naturally being uniquely me.
- I confess I am broken, and I rise from the ages as a golden phoenix.
- I confess I was broken by a bruise in childhood, but in healing, I have found my greatness.
- I confess how my heart was broken, witnessing rage and withdrawal of love. I confess my greatness, a great, huge heart filled with divine love.
- I confess my wounds, which do not trust. And I confess my greatness by embracing and overpowering love.
- I confess my wound of being a bother; my greatness is looking and finding the Eros of others and assisting them to see what I can uniquely see.
- I confess my wound of not feeling loved enough. I confess my greatness of offering compassion to others as I have learned to feel for myself.

The wound and the greatness, the holy and the broken *Hallelujah*. And that is what Leonard did not quite get—they are the same. **It's through my** broken *Hallelujah* **that I get to the holy** *Hallelujah.* There is no other path than the path through confessions of wound, happening and feeling them rise up, feeling them move and be transformed as I feel the brokenness become the wholeness.

> *It is only when I feel the intimate contours of my wounding that I can begin to stand against existential risk and stand for the healing of the planet.*

Even in our world of the human potential movement, when the wound isn't owned, destruction happens. Because we cannot own our malice, we cannot own our anger and rage—therefore we cannot transform it. "I Wanna Know What Love Is," Foreigner [*See Appendix*]

Evolutionary Church is the beginning of the beginning, and Evolutionary Church is the answer to existential risk. Innovation and interiors—it is this church; it is the new Renaissance.

Imagine that it is going to happen. Five million people across the world. Evolutionary Churches all over the world are self-organizing to higher levels of love, consciousness, and creativity.

What an honor to be with everyone. I could not think of any place we'd rather be.

Love you madly. *Amen.*

INDEX

abandoned 147
Abhinavagupta 152, 153
abyss 98, 126
Adonai 41
Advaita 134
alive 3, 15, 18, 24, 44, 70, 77, 79, 162, 169, 179
All-That-Is 42, 46, 83, 93, 98, 103, 123, 126, 148, 177, 178
allurement 62, 65, 66, 109, 118, 160, 162
Almaas 139, 140, 141, 142, 143
anochi 13, 97
arousal 28
atom 50, 173
atomic bomb 173
attraction 62, 65, 66, 160
Aurobindo, Sri 136
avodah 105
awaken xxxviii, 34, 37, 38, 41, 42, 48, 65, 84, 108, 124, 152
awakened xxxviii, 11, 38, 119
aware 9, 127, 133
awesomeness 12, 13, 22, 48, 135, 174

Ba'al 82
Baal Shem Tov 82
beauty 25, 32, 37, 69, 91, 111, 127, 167
Bethlehem 2, 21, 60, 62, 81, 134, 148
betrayal 81, 137
Big Bang 66, 67
brain 50, 116
breath 2, 70, 101, 107, 147

Brin, Sergei 162
Buddha, Gautama 17, 36, 52, 56, 178
Buddhism 75, 159
bypass 45, 64, 82, 83, 90, 134, 138, 143, 148, 154, 155, 169

calling xxxviii, xxxix, 13, 27, 38, 47, 81, 96, 103, 147, 148, 152, 164, 172, 173, 174
Camus 158
capacities 10, 68, 126
Capra, Fritjof 22
certainty 120, 124, 132
chain 62
chakra vii, 66, 78
chant 106, 143
chaos theory 42, 97, 175
Chetanananda 152
children 33, 35, 56, 99, 110, 115, 178
choice 151
Christ 8, 11, 18, 21, 41, 47, 48, 49, 50, 80, 84, 85, 87, 132, 174, 178
Christianity 75, 137, 159
Church 7, 12, 14, 17, 20, 21, 24, 29, 36, 39, 43, 45, 47, 61, 106, 107, 108, 112, 114, 115, 117, 118, 124, 127, 134, 138, 142, 147, 148, 149, 172, 181
circle 4, 35, 57, 73, 81, 98, 103, 105, 126, 177
clarity 51
co-creator 49, 163, 172, 173
codependency 94

INDEX

Cohen, Andrew 66
collapse 136
commitment 129, 130, 179
communion 18, 19, 47, 102, 131, 163
community 25, 53, 54, 77, 149, 164, 165, 178
complexity 22, 42, 97, 110, 166, 175, 178
confession 99, 112, 134, 175
connecting 29, 100, 164, 173, 174
Conscious Evolution 12, 31, 41, 46, 69, 79, 109, 152
consciousness 8, 10, 26, 37, 41, 42, 49, 66, 67, 68, 70, 82, 86, 87, 92, 127, 136, 149, 159, 160, 171, 176, 179, 181
contemplating 48
continuity of consciousness 49
contraction 15, 36, 71, 78
control 142
conversation viii, 119, 123
CosmoErotic Humanism 75
Cosmos viii, xxxviii, xxxix, 62, 63, 104, 110, 118, 119, 147, 153, 171, 178
creation xxxviii, xxxix, 1, 2, 7, 19, 20, 26, 28, 35, 38, 65, 66, 67, 68, 79, 84, 97, 112, 127, 128, 129, 163, 164, 174
creativity xxxviii, 19, 26, 27, 28, 29, 30, 63, 67, 68, 83, 85, 86, 101, 104, 131, 156, 160, 166, 167, 171, 172, 181
Creator 28, 49, 84, 113
crying 56, 77, 78, 101
culture 18, 70, 102, 166, 167

death 8, 49, 76, 77, 113, 132, 133, 135, 177
delight 42, 55, 84, 94, 136, 147, 148, 167, 168, 176, 177
democracy 175
democratizing enlightenment 154

denial 143
depression 16, 157, 158, 159
desire xxxviii, 37, 88, 89, 101, 102, 150, 151, 152, 153, 155, 156, 157, 160, 163
dharma viii, 13, 52
dignity 6, 13, 23, 24, 25, 45, 64, 82, 83, 84, 88, 90, 91, 97, 99, 170, 171
distinction 19, 51
divides 61
Divine xxxviii, xxxix, 11, 13, 14, 16, 17, 24, 25, 66, 102, 108, 114, 128, 136, 140, 141
divinity 63, 71, 114, 117, 122, 129, 141, 145, 155
dogma 3, 6, 98, 108, 109, 110
dreams 10, 150

Earth viii, 2, 25, 26, 37, 40, 41, 48, 49, 53, 57, 61, 67, 71, 80, 87, 100, 101, 102, 118, 133, 136, 144, 150, 156, 166, 173, 174
economics 174
ecstasy 25, 87, 109, 162
ego xxxviii, 17, 33, 34, 51, 52, 62, 64, 88, 139, 140, 141, 142, 163, 175
Egypt 170
Elohim 41
embodied iv, xxxviii, 49, 62, 65, 174
embracing 3, 87, 122, 180
emptiness 15, 140
enlightenment 123, 130, 133, 154
equation 103
Erhard, Werner 152
Eros 21, 22, 31, 34, 35, 36, 59, 60, 62, 70, 77, 90, 98, 126, 136, 176, 180

family 6, 7, 44, 54, 55, 94, 135, 179, 180
impulse xxxviii, 1, 2, 7, 8, 19, 23, 26, 28, 40, 60, 63, 67, 68, 69,

72, 77, 79, 80, 81, 86, 92, 96,
98, 105, 106, 133, 153, 156,
161, 162, 163, 173, 174
Love iii, vi, vii, viii, ix, xxxviii,
xxxix, 2, 6, 11, 16, 17, 18, 19,
20, 33, 34, 35, 37, 41, 44, 59,
60, 61, 62, 63, 64, 65, 66, 69,
70, 71, 72, 73, 74, 77, 78, 84,
85, 91, 95, 96, 97, 101, 105,
107, 112, 137, 138, 142, 149,
150, 151, 152, 153, 154, 156,
157, 159, 160, 162, 165, 172,
174, 181
partners 38, 39, 118, 164
Story xxxviii, xxxix, 9, 10, 11, 12,
13, 24, 25, 31, 33, 38, 39, 49,
52, 53, 55, 63, 65, 71, 74, 75,
84, 85, 100, 103, 108, 109,
118, 131, 133, 134, 135, 136,
137, 145, 154, 161, 162, 163,
167, 175, 176, 178
Unique Self vi, vii, viii, xxxviii,
xxxix, 2, 6, 10, 11, 12, 14, 15,
16, 17, 18, 20, 21, 25, 27, 28,
29, 30, 31, 36, 37, 38, 39, 40,
47, 48, 50, 51, 52, 57, 59, 60,
61, 71, 74, 77, 78, 79, 81, 84,
86, 87, 88, 94, 95, 96, 98, 100,
101, 102, 103, 104, 105, 106,
107, 112, 123, 130, 142, 143,
145, 147, 152, 156, 157, 158,
164, 165, 174, 175
erotic 22, 32, 35, 65, 66, 69, 72, 90,
180
Essential Self vii, 79, 80, 87, 174
ethnocentric 135, 171
ethos 139
evil 44, 141
evolution xxxviii, 1, 2, 9, 21, 22, 24,
30, 41, 46, 47, 49, 59, 60, 68,
69, 70, 72, 80, 92, 96, 97, 100,
102, 104, 107, 113, 114, 118,
125, 127, 131, 136, 138, 147,
151, 153, 156, 159, 161, 165,
172, 173
evolutionary xxxviii, xxxix, 1, 2, 4, 6,
7, 8, 22, 23, 27, 33, 46, 60, 62,
63, 66, 68, 70, 72, 75, 78, 79,
80, 81, 82, 83, 84, 85, 86, 87,
88, 91, 92, 93, 94, 97, 98, 100,
105, 106, 108, 111, 118, 125,
133, 138, 139, 151, 153, 156,
157, 160, 161, 162, 163, 164,
173, 174, 178
Evolutionary God 4
Evolutionary Love iii, xxxviii, xxxix,
2, 33, 96, 112, 150, 151, 152,
153, 154, 156, 157, 162, 164,
172, 174
existential risk 77, 81, 96, 123, 161,
177, 181
Eye 42
 of humanity xxxix, 7, 8, 26, 41, 46,
60, 87, 107, 127, 174
 of the Heart 101
 of the Spirit 42

faith 61
features 176
feelings 18, 41, 42, 59, 65, 73, 74, 84,
95, 132, 133, 139, 140, 141,
142, 143, 160, 162, 179, 180,
181
feminine 45, 68, 172, 173
Fiekowsky, Peter 10
Field 5, 62, 66, 69, 164
 of Reality vi, xxxviii, xxxix, 5, 7,
22, 23, 24, 33, 42, 43, 44, 45,
50, 62, 64, 65, 72, 78, 82, 83,
89, 90, 91, 93, 97, 99, 159, 162,
164, 180
First Principles 90
first shock of existence 177
forgiveness 49, 56, 132, 133
freedom 160
fulfilment 68

INDEX

fundamentalism 4, 44, 109, 111, 155, 171

gavoha 105
genius 11, 23, 28, 59, 87, 100, 101, 112, 173
gifts xxxix, 16, 37, 46, 48, 61, 72, 90, 95, 105, 112, 147
Global viii
  intimacy vi, viii, 3, 5, 6, 7, 15, 19, 20, 22, 24, 63, 97, 98, 99, 104, 110, 111, 131, 145, 155, 170, 171
  intimacy disorder viii
Global Action Paralysis xxxix
Goddess 97
Gospel 3
Griffin, David Ray iv, 22, 26, 27, 28, 36, 39, 45, 161
ground 120

Hallelujah vi, viii, 4, 5, 6, 24, 25, 44, 45, 46, 48, 57, 63, 64, 72, 83, 99, 100, 102, 108, 109, 110, 117, 124, 127, 135, 138, 148, 155, 169, 170, 171, 174, 181
Hasidic 82
heart xxxix, 2, 3, 4, 19, 20, 26, 40, 50, 58, 68, 69, 80, 94, 101, 104, 106, 140, 148, 149, 150, 151, 152, 154, 155, 156, 157, 160, 163, 176, 177, 178, 180
heartbreak xxxix, 2, 3, 4, 19, 20, 26, 40, 50, 58, 68, 69, 80, 94, 101, 104, 106, 140, 148, 149, 150, 151, 152, 154, 155, 156, 157, 160, 163, 176, 177, 178, 180
heaven 9, 56, 61, 71, 129, 155
Hebrew 12, 13, 53, 64, 122, 153
Homo amor 81
Homo sapiens 67, 86, 131, 143
Homo universalis 84, 86, 133
honor 45, 177, 181
Hubbard, Barbara Marx iii, iv, xxx-viii, 11, 12, 16, 17, 36, 43, 49, 50, 52, 53, 79, 94, 142
human vii, 70, 79, 80, 87, 92
humanity viii, 156
humans 67, 70, 81, 92, 93, 150

identified 49, 51
identify 52, 53, 57
identity 29, 81, 117, 142, 145, 151, 154, 156, 157, 158, 159, 160, 161, 177
illusion 35, 50, 100, 127, 131, 133, 139, 140, 141, 150
imagination 61, 167
imagine vii, 59, 60, 68, 89, 101, 103, 108, 161, 181
individual xxxix, 93, 100, 113, 114, 125, 140, 166, 168, 177
Infinity of Intimacy vi, 3, 5, 6, 7, 22, 24, 63, 97, 98, 99, 104, 110, 111, 145, 155, 170, 171
Infinity of Power 3, 6, 22, 63, 110, 145
influence 4, 57, 73, 81, 98, 103, 105, 126, 177
innocence 117, 145
Inside of the Inside 65, 100
integration 136, 141, 171
integrity 180
interior sciences 22, 33, 42, 97, 176
intimacy xxxviii, 2, 4, 6, 22, 24, 26, 28, 44, 57, 62, 73, 81, 96, 97, 98, 103, 104, 105, 110, 126, 131, 132, 134, 136, 138, 139, 140, 141, 144, 146, 148, 159, 161, 173, 177
intimate 22, 44, 63, 97, 103, 104, 137, 145, 146, 176, 181
Intimate Universe 22, 97, 103
irreducible 98, 123, 126, 130

Jerusalem 9, 10, 21, 132, 133, 134, 138
Jesus 8, 9, 18, 21, 36, 49, 51, 56, 85,

132, 133, 134, 137, 145, 172
joining genius 112, 173
joy 46, 81, 84, 87, 90, 95, 97, 112,
    134, 136, 145, 147, 148, 167,
    171, 177

Kabbalah 12, 13, 14, 32, 153, 178
kadisha 54
kamtzan 53
Kashmir Shaivism 153
Kempton, Sally 153
kiss 90
knowledge 107, 169
Kurzweil, Ray 60

Lainer, Mordechai 154
laughter 138
leaders 71
leadership 14, 71
leading 35, 57, 87, 107, 143, 163,
    164, 175
line 151, 155
loneliness 44, 64, 102
longing 101, 146, 165
Love iii, vi, vii, viii, ix, xxxviii, xxxix,
    2, 6, 11, 16, 17, 18, 19, 20, 33,
    34, 35, 37, 41, 44, 59, 60, 61,
    62, 63, 64, 65, 66, 69, 70, 71,
    72, 73, 74, 77, 78, 84, 85, 91,
    95, 96, 97, 101, 105, 107, 112,
    137, 138, 142, 149, 150, 151,
    152, 153, 154, 156, 157, 159,
    160, 162, 165, 172, 174, 181
  story xxxviii, xxxix, 9, 10, 11, 12,
    13, 24, 25, 31, 33, 38, 39, 49,
    52, 53, 55, 63, 65, 71, 74, 75,
    84, 85, 100, 103, 108, 109,
    118, 131, 133, 134, 135, 136,
    137, 145, 154, 161, 162, 163,
    167, 175, 176, 178
LoveIntelligence viii, 5, 23, 24, 43,
    65, 98, 99, 110, 123, 126, 147,
    164, 177

manifestation 80
marriage 49, 50, 87
masculine 68, 173
mashiach 122
materialism 109
mathematics 115
meditation vi, vii, 66, 78
memetic 33, 162
memory 132, 147
metamorphosis 8, 85
metaphor 141, 158, 161
Michelangelo 161
mind of God 1
miracle 11, 144
mitosis 23, 24, 28
model 31, 90, 147, 165, 179
modern 45, 109, 134, 139, 158, 171
modernity 158, 159
mother 44, 100, 101, 134, 135, 136,
    140, 141, 142, 146, 158, 170,
    172, 177
multi-cell 10
music 24
mystery 8, 138
mysticism 145

Nachman of Breslov 105
namah 41, 106
neighbor 49, 135
New Age 13, 16, 17, 23, 36, 70, 104,
    105, 106, 137, 148, 157, 161
new human 81, 84, 85, 105, 173
new humanity xxxix, 2, 81, 100, 157,
    166, 172
nirvana 154
noosphere 2, 37, 38, 40, 41, 87, 94,
    102, 107, 124, 178

Outrageous Acts of Love 18, 35, 37,
    105
Outrageous Love vii, viii, 2, 6, 11,
    16, 17, 33, 34, 41, 59, 60, 61,
    62, 63, 64, 65, 69, 70, 71, 72,
    73, 74, 77, 78, 84, 91, 97, 107,

INDEX

112, 137, 142, 149, 156

Page, Larry 162
pan-interiority 169
paradox 23
partial 122
particles 66, 69
particular 16, 21, 57, 73, 82, 88, 111, 121, 135, 141, 142, 168
pathological 51
Pentecost vi, 9, 10, 12
planetary birth 100
pleasure 93, 175
pointing-out instruction 4, 5, 43
post-tragic 81
power 7, 29, 31, 38, 39, 47, 49, 50, 68, 80, 81, 87, 91, 107, 111, 121, 123, 124, 125, 130, 132, 133, 141, 145, 146
premodern 158, 159, 160
promise 7, 11
prophet 10
pseudo-eros 21
pseudo-erotic 35
psychology 139, 159
purpose xxxviii, 18, 24, 69, 86, 92, 101, 110, 156

quantum 7

Radin, Dean 118
Rama 178
Ramakrishna 155, 170
ratzuf 3
Reality vi, vii, xxxviii, xxxix, 5, 6, 7, 22, 23, 24, 30, 33, 39, 40, 42, 43, 44, 45, 50, 61, 62, 64, 65, 72, 77, 78, 82, 83, 88, 89, 90, 91, 92, 93, 94, 97, 99, 100, 104, 105, 130, 134, 136, 149, 159, 162, 164, 170, 171, 176, 180
realization 81, 97, 98, 136, 139, 157, 161, 176, 177
reclaiming 7, 45, 108

reincarnation 136
relationship 82, 114, 117, 118, 120, 121, 171, 175
religion iv
remembering viii, 146
Renaissance 63, 81, 161, 181
resonance viii, 15, 40, 41, 44, 60, 80, 82, 86, 101, 103, 105, 106, 107, 111, 134, 141
resurrection 8, 9, 49, 79, 80, 81, 84, 85, 87, 133
revealed 8, 97, 133
revelation 11, 13
role mate 164
Rumi 3, 23, 71, 110

Sabbath 54, 55, 136
sacred xxxviii, 11, 23, 74, 91, 114, 115, 116, 120, 131
samsara 154
Sanderson, Alexis 152
sangha 17
second shock of existence 177
security 34, 68, 88
Self xxxix, 2, 17, 18, 20, 27, 28, 29, 30, 31, 35, 36, 40, 49, 50, 61, 71, 79, 85, 86, 88, 96, 98, 100, 103, 104, 117, 120, 121, 123, 124, 125, 131, 134, 139, 140, 141, 142, 144, 145, 146, 148, 158, 175, 176, 180, 181
  organizing vii, 59
  realization 81, 97, 98, 136, 139, 157, 161, 176, 177
separate self 88, 139, 175
separation xxxix, 29, 38, 49, 87, 131, 132, 133, 140, 141, 142, 144, 146, 147, 150
sexual 22, 88
sexuality 90, 113, 180
shadow 31, 51, 170
shame 168
shards 12

Shekhinah 17
shever 170
shevirat 154
shiva 41, 106
shivaya 41, 106
siach 122
Solomon 3
soul mate 164
Source xxxix, 42, 46, 79, 91, 97, 133, 138, 139, 140, 141, 142, 143, 146, 147, 153, 158, 168, 171
source code 46, 138
Spirit 4, 10, 67, 80
Stein, Zak iii
story vi, vii, 44, 46, 47, 66, 74, 104, 159, 160, 162
St. Paul 8
structure of Reality 162
structures 97, 142
Sufism 53
suicide 147
Swimme, Brian 67
synagogue 61, 112, 152

tachat 3
tantra 42, 90
Taylor, Charles 158
temple 3, 170
tenderness 32
teshuva 65
The whole xxxix, 18, 25, 26, 27, 28, 33, 40, 41, 42, 48, 50, 65, 67, 71, 77, 79, 80, 85, 94, 99, 100, 101, 103, 107, 108, 124, 133, 142, 143, 151, 157, 162, 175
tikkun 50
traditions 65, 75
tragic 81
transcending 49
transformation xxxviii, xxxix, 11, 14, 51, 61, 81, 83, 85, 96, 120, 125, 133, 142, 161, 167, 169, 170, 178

transmission xxxviii, 154
True Self 134
truth 33, 42, 84, 88, 108, 109, 110, 128, 129, 130, 132, 135, 141, 160, 162
tvam 123
tzorech 105

uncertainty 109, 110
unconscious 133, 134
understanding 14, 115, 116, 118, 138
unique gift 14, 26, 27, 29, 40, 41, 47, 50, 52, 53, 57, 72, 81, 82, 98, 103, 111, 126, 159, 164, 177
uniqueness xxxix, 30, 40, 63, 88, 89, 96, 101, 107, 111, 123, 126, 140, 155, 174
Unique Self vi, vii, viii, xxxviii, xxxix, 2, 6, 10, 11, 12, 14, 15, 16, 17, 18, 20, 21, 25, 27, 28, 29, 30, 31, 36, 37, 38, 39, 40, 47, 48, 50, 51, 52, 57, 59, 60, 61, 71, 74, 77, 78, 79, 81, 84, 86, 87, 88, 94, 95, 96, 98, 100, 101, 102, 103, 104, 105, 106, 107, 112, 123, 130, 142, 143, 145, 147, 152, 156, 157, 158, 164, 165, 174, 175
Unique Self Symphony vi, vii, viii, xxxix, 2, 6, 10, 12, 14, 16, 18, 20, 21, 25, 27, 28, 29, 30, 31, 36, 37, 38, 39, 40, 47, 48, 50, 51, 57, 59, 60, 61, 71, 77, 78, 81, 84, 86, 87, 94, 95, 96, 100, 101, 102, 104, 105, 107, 123, 156, 157, 165, 174
Universe vii, viii, xxxix, 3, 15, 33, 44, 49, 59, 61, 66, 67, 69, 86, 87, 97, 104, 109, 118, 123, 159, 160, 161, 162, 176

vayar 170
victimized 145
visionary 102, 131

wake 147
watch 37, 144
WeSpace 95
Wheel of Co-Creation 164
where we are 62
whole mate 36, 164
whole, the xxxix, 18, 25, 26, 27, 28,
    33, 40, 41, 42, 48, 50, 65, 67,
    71, 77, 79, 80, 85, 94, 99, 100,
    101, 103, 107, 108, 124, 133,
    142, 143, 151, 157, 162, 175
who we are 86, 120, 128, 151
Wilber, Ken 52, 152
win/lose 23
World War II 44

xenophobic 21

yearning 19, 80, 96, 131, 143, 146,
    147, 151, 156, 162, 163, 165
Yom Kippur 74
Yossele 53, 54, 55, 56, 57

Zohar 17

Volume 3 — From Pain to Purpose

LIST OF EPISODES

1. Episode 21 — March 18, 2017
2. Episode 22 — March 25, 2017
3. Episode 23 — April 1, 2017
4. Episode 24 — April 8, 2017
5. Episode 25 — April 15, 2017
6. Episode 26 — April 22, 2017
7. Episode 27 — April 29, 2017
8. Episode 28 — May 6, 2017
9. Episode 29 — May 13, 2017
10. Episode 30 — May 20, 2017

www.ingramcontent.com/pod-product-compliance
Lightning Source LLC
LaVergne TN
LVHW011153080426
835508LV00007B/373